BHUTAN

The four guardians of the orients
(Mural painting, Dungtse Lhakhang, Paro)

The four guardians of the orients called "Gyelchen shi", or Four Great Kings, are almost always represented in the entry vestibules of temples, monasteries and dzongs. The guardian of the North is Namtoese. He holds a banner in his right hand and a mongoose spitting jewels in his left hand. The guardian of the West is Chenmisang. He holds a small chorten in his right hand. The guardian of the South is Phakyepo. He holds a sword in his right hand and his left rests on the scabbard. The guardian of the East, Yulkhorsung, is playing the lute. Each guardian has his particular headgear and is usually painted in a distinguishing colour: yellow for the north, red for the west, green for the south and white for the east. In some instances, however, all the guardians are painted in gold, as they are here. Gold is considered superior to all the others in the hierarchy of colours, and it carries regal connotations.

Photographs   Guy van Strydonck

Texts   Françoise Pommaret-Imaeda
Yoshiro Imaeda

BHUTAN
A Kingdom of
the Eastern Himalayas

English translation   Ian Noble

Publisher   **Shambhala • Boston • 1989**

SHAMBHALA PUBLICATIONS, INC.
Horticultural Hall
300 Massachusetts Avenue
Boston, Massachusetts 02115

Distributed in the United States by Random House and in Canada by Random House of Canada Ltd.

Library of Congress Cataloging in Publication Data

Strydonck, Guy van.
   Bhutan, a kingdom of the eastern Himalayas.
   Reprint. Originally published: Geneva: Editions
Olizane, 1984.
   Bibliography: p.
   1. Bhutan.   I. Pommaret-Imaeda, Françoise.
II. Imaeda, Yoshiro.   III. Title.
DS485.B503S77   1985   954.9'8   84-23610
ISBN-0-87773-321-X

Printed in Barcelona, Spain, by Cayfosa

Acknowledgement

I AM DEEPLY GRATEFUL TO HER MAJESTY Ashi Kesang Wangchuck, Queen Mother of Bhutan, for Her Majesty's generous hospitality and kindness as well as for the interest Her Majesty showed in the production of this book. Without the Queen Mother's encouragements this book would never have been published.

My deepest gratitude goes also to the members of the Royal Family, the Royal Government the Royal Body Guards, the Royal Bhutan Army, and to the various monks, officials and many friends for their kind hospitality. They spared neither time nor effort to make our stay in Bhutan so fascinating and enjoyable.

A special word of thanks is offered to Dasho Lhendup Dorji who so carefully planned and organised our visits to the most interesting places.

I would also like to express my thanks to Major Rinzin Dorji of the Royal Body Guards and Lt. Kesang of the Royal Bhutan Army who proved to be perfect cicerones as well as capable organisers and most congenial travelling companions.

The same thanks are extended to the Ven. Mynak Rinpoche, Director, and Mrs. Chime Wangmo, curator, of the National Museum of Bhutan and to Mr. Jacques Hainard, curator, and Mrs. Marceline de Montmollin, adviser, of the Ethnological Museum of Neuchâtel for having allowed me to take pictures of their collections and use them in this book.

Last but not least, my most sincere thanks go to my friends Françoise Pommaret-Imaeda and Yoshiro Imaeda for having undertaken the formidable task of writing the texts for this book and also for their help in selecting the pictures which illustrate it.

May all my many Bhutanese friends whom I have been unable to name here consider the gratitude expressed in this acknowledgment as being also addressed to them.

To all Bhutanese and to all readers of this book I beg for forgiveness for having rendered so imperfectly the incomparable beauties and treasures of Bhutan.

TASHIDELEK

Guy van Strydonck
Antwerp, spring 1984

5

Foreword

by Her Majesty
The Queen Mother of Bhutan

I AM EXTREMELY HAPPY that our dear friend Guy van Strydonck is making a new illustrated book on Bhutan. I know of no-one more suitable than Guy to produce this book as he is not only a highly talented and artistic photographer, but he also knows Bhutan well, and has a deep love and appreciation for our country and its rich and precious traditions and cultural heritage.

Mrs. Françoise Pommaret-Imaeda and Mr. Yoshiro Imaeda have made a valuable contribution in writing the text.

The Kingdom of Bhutan has been known from ancient times as "The Hidden Holy Land" (Beyul) traversed and richly blessed by Guru Padma Sambhava in the eighth century, and later blessed by many great saints like Kunkhen Longchen, Phajo Drugom, Drukpa Kunley, Ngawang Chogyel and the great Shabdrung Ngawang Namgyel.

During several centuries of self imposed isolation from the outside world, prompted largely by political considerations, the Kingdom of Bhutan developed its own social economic and political institutions and a philosophy of life which have imparted stability, strength and resilience to Bhutanese society over the ages.

In a natural environment of beauty, peace and tranquillity, cultural and spiritual values have grown and flourished.

Guy's exquisite photographs have captured the rhythm, the peace and harmony, the essence of my country and people.

Kesang Wangchuck.

Her Majesty, The Queen Mother of Bhutan

Contents

Introduction

BHUTAN REMAINS SO LITTLE-KNOWN, so surrounded in mystery, and has such a wide variety of landscape and people that to describe it in a few short pages is perhaps a hopeless task and we sincerely hope our Bhutanese friends will forgive us any omissions or errors that may have cropped up in this introduction.

TWO PORTUGUESE JESUITS, Father Cacella and Cabral, are believed to be the first westerners to enter Bhutan. In 1627 they spent several months with the Shabdrung Ngawang Namgyel whom they described as "the King and at the same time the chief Lama".

The 18th and 19th centuries saw the arrival of the British, well established in India. Several British missions were sent to Bhutan to seek trading privileges and, in particular, a right of passage for goods between Tibet and India. Missions led by Bogle and Hamilton (1774-75), by Hamilton (1776 and 1777) and by Turner and Davis (1783) were characterized by mutual understanding and generally good relations between Bhutanese and British. However, in the 19th century, things turned sour and successive missions by Bose (1815), Pemberton (1838) and above all by Eden (1863-64) saw increasing animosity between the two countries which led, in 1864-65, to the Duar War.

During the 20th century only a few politicians - including Cl. White who was a British Political Officer in Sikkim - and other public figures came to Bhutan by invitation and some wrote accounts of their trips.

For three and a half centuries, Bhutan was thus only known to the outside world through often impressionistic accounts of these travellers. When Bhutan joined the United Nations in 1971, and was subsequently opened up to tourists in 1974, the popular image of the country portrayed it either as a kind of Shangri-La or as one of the least-developed nations in the world. Such clichés do not do justice to the extraordinary ethnic and geographical diversity of the country, which has a long and rich history and great pride in its customs. Under the influence of its fourth king, His Majesty Jigme Singye Wangchuck, Bhutan is striving to achieve a harmonious compromise between tradition and economic development.

THE CENTURIES-OLD ISOLATION OF BHUTAN may be explained in part by the country's geography. Located between India and China, its 47,000 square kilometres of territory form a gigantic staircase between the narrow lowland region of the south approx. 300 metres above sea-level and the lofty Himalayan peaks of the north over 7,000 metres high. The central valleys - the most densely populated region - are very difficult to reach from the south because of a 2,000 metre-high chain of mountains interspersed with unhealthy jungle-covered gorges. These previously made access both dangerous and difficult. Paradoxically, until the border with Tibet was closed in 1959, the high Himalayas gave easy access through certain mountain passes, and there was a considerable amount of trade between the two countries. These three relief zones, the Foothills, Inner and High Himalayas, also define three climatic regions: tropical, temperate with monsoon, and alpine.

These climatic variations, coupled with the dramatic changes in altitude, make Bhutan a country with an extremely rich flora. Over a mere 70 kilometres one passes from rice paddies, banana and orange groves at 1,300 metres in the Punakha region, through a deciduous forest and then an alpine forest (at Gasa), finally arriving in the Laya region where yaks are raised and only barley and winter wheat can be grown.

Southern Bhutan consists of often impenetrable jungles full of tropical trees and fruits. In the central valleys apples, peaches, plums and apricots can be found, and rhododendrons grow side by side with fir trees, blue pines and oaks. An infinite variety of plants and flowers grow on the slopes and in the valleys, giving Bhutan its centuries-old name: "Southern Valleys of Medicinal Herbs".

The fauna also varies with the different types of vegetation. Elephants, tigers, buffaloes and snakes abund in the southern forests, while the central Himalayan region is full of pheasants, monkeys, wild boars and above all fearsome black bears. The desolate high valleys are the home of yaks, of the retiring blue sheep and the extremely rare snow leopard.

Differing ethnic groups are also distributed according to the varying environments. Southern Bhutan is inhabited mainly by Nepalese farmers who arrived in the country at the end of the 19th century and are now fully integrated Bhutanese citizens.

Small trading towns, such as Phuntsholing, Gaylegphug and Samdrup Jongkhar, prosper in this region on the Indian border. These towns boast small-scale industries, such as match factories, fruit juice and jam processing units, a distillery and two cement plants.

The central Himalayan region is the home of the *Drukpa* people, who are of Mongoloid origin. Most breed cattle or cultivate the land and their dwellings are spread over a wide area, with small towns growing around the *dzongs*, or fortified monasteries, which used to defend each valley. The appearance of these towns is directly linked to the improvement in communications and to the formation of a middle class of civil servants and shopkeepers.

The northern Himalayan zone, over 3,000 metres, is the haunt of semi-nomadic yak herdsmen. They spend most of the year in their black tents woven from yak hair, but also possess drystone-walled houses, where they spend the coldest months of the year and which are used to store their goods. Precious additives to a diet composed mainly of yak milk, butter, cheese and meat are barley and winter wheat, plus a few root vegetables which they grow in small fields.

This horizontal division of Bhutan into three ecological zones (northern, central and southern) would only give a very approximate idea of the country's ethnic and geographical diversity if we do not also consider its vertical divisions. In fact the mountain chains which divide the central valleys all run from north to south and form real barriers between different parts of the country - barriers which are perceived as such by the people themselves. The central Himalayan region can thus be divided longitudinally into three parts which are each distinct but which are all inhabited by the *Drukpas*, who speak languages of the Tibeto-Burmese group.

Western Bhutan is made up of the valleys of Haa (2,700 metres above sea-level), Paro (2,200 metres), Thimphu (2,300 metres) and Punakha and Wangdiphodrang (1,300 metres). With the exception of Haa valley, whose rigourous climate suits it more for animal breeding and which used to be very involved in trading with Tibet, western Bhutan is a region of rice-paddies and orchards. All types of vegetables and fruit flourish in the fertile valleys, and the relative wealth of the inhabitants can be inferred from their very large houses, in which several generations co-habit. The walls are formed of dried mud, and the upper floors of the houses are remarkable wood-structures, frequently beautifully painted.

Traditionally wooden shingles were used for roofing but these have in some cases been replaced by corrugate iron. Fortunately, slate being mined from rich local deposits may again provide roofing material which enhances the traditional architecture.

The mountain slopes are covered by rich coniferous and deciduous forests where forestry is strictry regulated, since Bhutan recognizes what a precious asset its woodlands are. All the valleys are strewn with reminders of the past, in particular with monasteries and fortresses. Since the fifties, the country's capital has been located in the Thimphu valley. The five valleys which make up western Bhutan are where *Dzongkha*, the "language of the Dzong (fortress)" is spoken. It has become the official language of Bhutan. Although similar to Tibetan, it has many differences especially in the pronounciation and conjugation of verbs.

The boundary between eastern and western Bhutan is generally taken to be a 3,300 metre-high pass through the Black Mountains (5,000 metres) called Pele-la. Central Bhutan is made up of two valleys: Tongsa and Bumthang, plus the more southerly district of Khyeng, famous for its bamboo work. Khyeng is also the home of several isolated aboriginal tribes known as *Monpas* and considered by the Bhutanese as the first inhabitants of their country.

Tongsa (2,200 metres above sea-level) hardly deserves to be called a valley. It is in reality a gorge cut out by the Mangde river, with a few cultivated areas cut into its steep slopes. Tongsa is best known for its fortress, which is perhaps the most impressive in the country.

A 3,300 metre-high pass, the Yuto-la, leads to Bumthang which is a group of four valleys at altitudes from 2,700 to 4,000 metres: Chume and Choekhor which are mainly agricultural and Tang and Ura where yak and sheep herding are carried out. Bumthang is proud of its rich historical and artistic traditions and of its language which is close to that of Kurtoe in the north-east, and which still contains many archaic features. Religious traditions are very much alive here and each monastery, each holy place, is the focus of long tales in which reality and myth are closely interwoven. As in western Bhutan, the mountains are covered with dense forests but the cold climate precludes rice cultivation. Even though rice brought in from other valleys is eaten, buckwheat cakes are the staple food. In Bumthang, houses are made not of dried mud but of stone, but one finds the elaborate woodwork on the upper floors and the unique sloping roofs which are characteristic of Bhutanese architecture.

The Thumshing-la pass, over 4,000 metres high, separates central from eastern Bhutan. The latter consists of the Kurtoe, Mongar and Tashigang regions, plus that part of southern Bhutan adjacent to the Indian border. The eastern region is the land of the *Sharchops* - the "people of the east" - who speak their own language known as *Sharchopkha*. The climate there is generally warmer and drier, and the slopes barer than in the west. It is a region of deep valleys which often consist of no more than the river itself, with fields and houses clinging to their steep slopes. Rice, wheat and barley are cultivated widely but corn (maize) is the staple crop and numerous cattle may be seen grazing by the sides of the roads. Most of the houses follow the traditional Bhutanese pattern, in stone and wood, but toward the south some are made of bamboo matting and are raised up on piles.

The *Sharchops* are well known for their piety, and the region is dotted with small temples where *gomchens*, laymen trained in religious practices, live with their families away from monastic commmunities. The women are unequalled in their skill at weaving beautiful fabrics of raw silk - known as *bura* - and of cotton with infinitely varied designs.

Two days on foot to the east of Tashigang fortress, one finds the astonishing valley of Sakteng, 3,000 metres above sea-level, and virtually unknown to the outside world. This book contains several photographs of the valley, which will be described in more detail in chapter 5. For the moment, we will simply mention that the inhabitants of the valley, sometimes known as *Brogpas* (shepherds), *Dakpas* or *Daps* are herdsmen and are related to the peoples known as *Monpas*, from the Tawang region of Arunachal Pradesh in N.E. India.

BHUTAN IS MADE UP OF A MOSAIC of varied populations which, right up to the present day, have lived in valleys isolated from one another by formidable mountain passes and cut off from the outside world by mountain barriers which are extremely difficult to cross. And yet this is a country which is a real nation of one million inhabitants united in the same desire for stability and peace and who share the same pride in being Bhutanese. This keen sense of belonging to the Bhutanese nation is rooted in a mutual respect for the cultural values of each of the peoples which the forces of history have formed into the Bhutanese nation.

Stone implements found in Bhutan seem to indicate that the country was inhabited fairly early, probably around 2000 B.C. Moreover, the relatively large number of megaliths to be seen today may have been used to mark out territories or for ritual practices. However, it is difficult to draw conclusions concerning the prehistory of Bhutan, since almost no archeological research has yet been carried out.

As for the history of Bhutan, this was for centuries so closely bound up with the religious history of the country that the religious school which became dominant from the 17th century, the Drukpa school, gave its name to the country and its inhabitants: in Dzongkha, Bhutan is called *Druk-yul* and the Bhutanese people *Drukpas*. A more poetic translation is often given: "Druk-yul" also means "Land of the Dragon", and this is explained by the following anecdote: when Tsangpa Gyare Yeshe Dorje (1161-1211) was consecrating a new monastery in Central Tibet at the end of the 12th century, he heard the thunder which popular belief holds to be the voice of the dragon ("druk"). He therefore decided to name this monastery "Druk", and so the religious school which he founded was called "Drukpa". Bhutan's other traditional names are *Lhomon Khashi* or "The Southern Mon(pa) Country of Four Approaches".

The origin of the present name of Bhutan is unclear. One interpretation is that it comes from the Indian term *Bhotanta* which refers to all those regions bordering on Tibet.

IN ORDER TO PROVIDE A BRIEF SKETCH of the history of Bhutan up to the end of the 19th century, we must consider the main religious figures who were not only important in their own time but who live on in the minds and memories of the people today.

Bhutanese tradition has it that a tantrist of Indian birth, Padmasambhava or Pemajungne, also known as Guru Rinpoche and considered by the Nyingmapa or "Old" school as their spiritual master and as the Second Buddha, came to Bhutan in the 8th century A.D. As in Tibet, he introduced Buddhism in its tantric form. All the places he visited and in which he meditated are places of pilgrimage for the Bhutanese, who also worship his Eight Manifestations in almost all the temples in the country. The history of the conversion to Buddhism of a king reigning in Bumthang indicates that at the time of Padmasambhava the valleys of Bhutan were already inhabited by a population who practised an animistic type of religion but whose origin remains a mystery.

After this first introduction of Buddhism and probably the first migrations from Tibet, the 9th and 10th centuries form a period of great obscurity. Following the assassination of the anti-Buddhist King Langdarma of Tibet in A.D. 842, Tibet itself plunged into great political turmoil and Buddhism almost completely disappeared, surviving only in remote regions. We have no information about Bhutan in the course of these troubled centuries, but it is plausible to imagine that many emigrants fled from Tibet into the valleys of Bhutan at this time.

The 11th century saw the revival of Buddhism in Bhutan, this was the period of the activity of the *tertons* or "discoverers of treasures" in Paro and Bumthang. These treasures were usually texts hidden by Padmasambhava and other saints and discovered by the predestined *tertons* at a favourable moment.

The end of the 11th century and the beginning of the 12th saw a period of religious expansion in Tibet and a number of different religious schools came into being including the Kadampa, Kagyupa and Sakyapa schools. The missionary activity of these new schools was also directed at the "Southern Valleys", and at the end of the 12th century, Gyelwa Lhanangpa (1164-1224) arrived in western Bhutan. He was the founder of the Lhapa school, a branch of the Kagyupa school, and had special links with the valley of Paro, since he had inherited land in this fertile region from his great-great-grandfather. He accordingly established the Lhapa school in western Bhutan.

In the first half of the 13th century, a monk by the name of Phajo Drugom Shigpo (1184-1211) arrived in Bhutan. He belonged to another branch of the Kagyupa, the Drukpas, founded by Tsangpa Gyare Yeshe Dorje (1161-1211). He came to Bhutan following a prophecy of Tsangpa Gyare who ordered him to go to the South. As soon as he arrived, Phajo Drugom Shigpo came into conflict with the Lhapas, who were already firmly established in western Bhutan. However, Phajo Drugom Shigpo finally won his struggle with the Lhapas and, having married a woman from the Thimphu valley, he founded the first Drukpa monasteries at Phajoding and Tango. The Lhapa school nevertheless continued until the 17th century when it was totally crushed by the Shabdrung Ngawang Namgyel. However, many monks, whether belonging to the Drukpa school or not, continued to come to Bhutan between the 12th and the 17th centuries. Barawa (1320-1391), for example, founded a sub-sect of the Drukpas and had a monastery at Brangyekha in the Paro valley. In the same way, the distinctive Nenyingpa school founded several monasteries in western Bhutan, amongst which was Dzongdrakha in the Paro valley.

Longchen Rabjampa (1308-1363), the great philosopher of the Nyingmapa school, went to Bumthang where he founded the monasteries of Tharpaling, Samtenling and Shinkar and in 1355 wrote an eulogy on the valley of Bumthang.

In the 15th century a man arrived in western Bhutan who is unquestionably the most popular of the religious figures: Drukpa Kunley, "the divine madman" (1455-1529). All Bhutanese are familiar with his adventures. In fact, he belonged to the Drukpa school and to the princely family of Gya, from which came the successive abbots of Ralung, one of the main Drukpa monasteries. His wandering life style, the eccentric and shocking behaviour with which he taught the essence of religion and his songs give him a special place in the history of tantric buddhism. His descendants became equally famous in Bhutan, especially Tenzin Rabgye (1638-1696) who was the famous 4th Temporal Ruler (*Desi* or *Deb*) of Bhutan.

Although only monks who came from Tibet to Bhutan have so far been mentioned, it should not be forgotten that from the 14th century onwards many eminent monks were born on Bhutanese soil.

The most famous among them is Pema Lingpa, a descendant of Gyalwa Lhanangpa, who was born in Bumthang in 1450 and died there in 1521. Pema Lingpa, however, did not belong to the Lhapa school but to the Nyingmapa school, which was very powerful in central Bhutan. He was the reincarnation not only of Guru Rinpoche but also of the great Nyingmapa scholar Longchen Rabjampa. Pema Lingpa, in addition to his activities as a *terton* or discoverer of treasures, founded the temples of Petsheling, Tamshing and Kunzangbrag in Bumthang. He was the originator of a number of sacred dances, which came to him in visions, and he also left behind him important writings. He is intimately linked to the history of the Bumthang valley, where his memory has left traces everywhere. His descendants played an important role in the development of the Nyingmapa school and one of them set up Gangtey monastery, built on the borders of central and western Bhutan in the Black Mountains.

THIS BRIEF OUTLINE indicates how Bhutan was an important area of missionary activity for the religious schools between the 12th and the beginning of the 17th centuries, but it also highlights the lack of political unity which characterized Bhutan during this period.

It was in the 17th century that Bhutan became a unified state, thanks to the political and religious charisma of Ngawang Namgyel (1594-1651) of the Drukpa school. He took the honorary title of Shabdrung, "at whose feet one submits" but his history is too long to be told in detail and we shall limit ourselves to its broad outlines.

In 1616, Shabdrung Ngawang Namgyel, fleeing from Tibet, arrived in western Bhutan. He had been born into the princely Gya family and he was the 18th abbot of Ralung, a great Drukpa monastery. He had been recognized as the incarnation of the famous Drukpa scholar Pema Karpo (1527-1592) but this recognition had been challenged by the Tsang Desi, the head of the province of Tsang in Tibet, who had his own candidate. Under these circumstances, Ngawang Namgyel was obliged to flee from Ralung and to take refuge in western Bhutan, where, as we have seen, the Drukpa school was firmly established. Shabdrung Ngawang Namgyel accordingly went to the valleys of Thimphu and Paro, where his great-great-grandfather Ngawang Choegyel (1465-1540) had founded the monasteries of Panri Zampa and Druk Choeding respectively. In the upper Thimphu valley, the Shabdrung himself founded the monastery of Cheri in 1619, and in 1629 he founded his first dzong, Simtokha, near Thimphu.

The system of dzongs built in each valley not only symbolized the might of the Drukpa school, since each dzong contained a monastery, but also constituted an unrivalled instrument of governement and unification of the country. However, before he could bring about the unification of Bhutan, the Shabdrung had to fight against his enemies both at home and abroad. His foreign enemies were the Tibetans, whose army was first organized by the Tsang Desi in order to invade Bhutan. Their first attempt, which took place shortly after the arrival of the Shabdrung, was repelled, and their renewed attacks in 1634 and 1639 met with no greater success. In 1645 and 1648, the Tibetans, now aided by the Mongol army which supported the new

Tibetan government of the 5th Dalai Lama, made further fruitless attempts at conquest.

The enemies of the Shabdrung at home were the "five groups of lamas", in other words the religious schools which had long been established in Bhutan and against which the Shabdrung had fought in order to consolidate his own power and that of the Drukpa school. The Shabdrung gave Bhutan a system of laws based on the unwritten laws then in common use, established a state monk-body under a religious leader, the *Je Khenpo* and a theocracy administered by monks at whose head he put a temporal leader, the *Desi*. This dual system of government, known as *choesi*, was unified and transcended in the person of the Shabdrung Ngawang Namgyel.

In 1651, the Shabdrung went into retreat in Punakha dzong and died while he was there. His death was kept a secret for over half a century. The reasons for this concealment no doubt lie in the concern to avoid turmoil - in a nation which had only just come into existence - which might have broken out before a worthy successor to the Shabdrung could be found.

I T WAS IN THE FIRST HALF OF THE 18TH CENTURY that the theory of the triple incarnation of the Body, Speech and Mind of the Shabdrung was finally established. However, only the successive "mental" incarnations were recognized as successors of the Shabdrung as heads of state. Hierarchically inferior to the incarnation of the Shabdrung, to whom the British gave the name *Dharma Raja*, came the head of the monk-body, the *Je Khenpo* and the temporal ruler, the *Desi* (or *Deb Raja* as the British called him). They continued the dual system of government which was to last until the coming of the monarchy at the beginning of 20th century.

The heads of dzongs (*Dzongpons*) were put in charge of the provinces. Some of these (at Daga, Tongsa and Paro) were more important than others and were given the title of *Penlop*. In the course of the 18th and the 19th centuries, these regional governors increased their powers to the detriment of the central government. Moreover, the dual system of government favoured political inertia and encouraged inter-factional struggles. These factors led to instability and increasingly frequent internal disputes which broke out into civil wars.

Beyond its frontiers, the government was faced with a new factor in the form of British hegemony in Assam and British colonial ambitions in the Himalayas. In the 18th century, British missions, seeking preferential trading relations with Tibet and Bhutan, were successful in establishing good relations between the Bhutanese and the British, without however the concrete results for which the latter had been hoping. The conflicting interests of the Bhutanese and the British over the question of the Duars rapidly tarnished these good relations and the expeditions in the 19th century bore signs of hostility. Continual skirmishes on the southern border from the 1830's onwards reached such proportions in 1864 that what is known as the Duar War took place. In November 1865, the treaty of Sinchula brought the war to an end and re-established normal relation. Bhutan gave up its rights over the Duars and in exchange received an annual allowance from the British.

The progressive weakening of the central government became more marked at the end of the 19th century and coincided with the emergence of the power of the two main governors in Paro and Tongsa, who had *de facto* control over western and central Bhutan. The struggle for power between these two governors came to a head in 1904 at the time of the British expedition to Tibet under Younghusband. Whilst the Penlop of Paro was determined to side with Tibet, which was already in the Chinese zone of influence, the Tongsa Penlop, Ugyen Wangchuck, advised by Kazi Ugyen Dorji, was in favour of increased cooperation with the British. Ugyen Wangchuck became the intermediary in negotiations between the Tibetans and the British and won the respect and confidence of the latter. He therefore came to be seen as the strong leader which Bhutan needed after so much instability.

ON 17TH DECEMBER 1907, Ugyen Wangchuck was unanimously elected as the first King of Bhutan by a constituent assembly made up of representatives of the monastic community, civil servants and the people. This marked the end of the dual system of government and the beginning of the hereditary monarchy which was to guarantee stability to the country. Ugyen Wangchuck died in 1926 and was succeeded by his son Jigme Wangchuck who reigned until his death in 1952.

The twenty-year reign of the third King, Jigme Dorji Wangchuck (1952-1972), was marked by the gradual opening up of the country to the outside world and by economic and social development. He was the father of modern Bhutan and an enlightened monarch. Amongst his achievements was Bhutan's entry into the United Nations in 1971.

His son, His Majesty Jigme Singye Wangchuck, today pursues the late King's policy of socio-economic progress. Bhutan now has a seat in a number of international organizations and UN agencies which provide aid for its development. These include the United Nations Development Programme, UNESCO, UNICEF, the FAO and the WHO. Other aid comes from the World Bank, the Asian Development Bank, the Asia and Pacific Economic and Social Commission and the Colombo Plan. Finally, Bhutan is a member of the Nonaligned Movement and of the South Asia Regional Cooperation.

The system of government is that of a monarchy. His Majesty the King is the Head of State and the Head of the Government. He is aided by the Cabinet, which is the main executive body and consists of the members of the Royal Advisory Council and the Ministers of Home Affairs, Foreign Affairs, Communications and Tourism, Social Services, Finance, Trade and Industry, plus other high-ranking officials.

The Royal Advisory Council (*Lodoe Tshogde*), set up in 1965, consists of the Chairman, appointed by the King, five representatives of the people, two representatives of the clergy, two representatives from southern Bhutan and a women's representative. They have a five-year mandate.

The National Assembly (*Tshongdu*) is the main legislative body. It was created in 1953 and consists of 150 members who fall into three categories:
- one hundred representatives of the people, elected for 3 years.
- ten representatives of the Clergy, elected by the State monastic community.
- forty representatives of the government, appointed by the King. These consist of the members of the Cabinet and various officials.

The National Assembly, presided over by the King, meets twice a year in Tashichho Dzong in Thimphu with sessions of variable length, depending on the importance of the subjects being dealt with.

The Je Khenpo is the head of the monk-body, which includes the central and regional State monastic communities. It should be mentioned that Bhutan is the only independent country in which Mahayana Buddhism is practised as the State religion.

Bhutan is divided up into eighteen administrative districts (*Dzongkhags*) under the control of the Ministry of Home Affairs and headed by a *Dzongda* and a *Dzongda wogma*, his deputy. Each district is in turn subdivided and the subdivisions are each headed by a *Dungpa*, aided by the village headmen (*Gaps*) who are elected for three years. Each Gap controls several villages and provides the link between the State administration and the villagers.

Judicial power is held in the last resort by the King, to whom all the Bhutanese may appeal. A High Court has its seat in Thimphu, and all the districts have a local court presided over by a magistrate or *Thrimpon*. The Bhutanese are tenaciously litigious, but the major crimes which afflict other societies are virtually non-existent.

THE ECONOMIC DEVELOPMENT of Bhutan has, since 1961, taken place in stages corresponding to five-year plans, with the sixth such plan now under way. The last twenty-five years have been marked by the efforts which have been made to bring about structural transformations in the socio-economic system, in other words to change a barter economy into a modern economy.

The Planning Commission centralizes all economic data and advises as to which options should be given priority.

The economy of Bhutan is still essentially based on agriculture and cattle-rearing. Ninety per cent of the population live from these activities. The main crops are maize, rice, wheat, barley, buckwheat, mustard and peppers. Cultivation of some recently-introduced cash crops has undergone remarkable expansion: to a certain extent asparagus and mushrooms, but above all potatoes, oranges, apples, cardamom, ginger and tropical fruits, as well as high-quality seeds. A huge programme for the development of irrigation is under way which will enable previously unused land to be cultivated. Because of its low population, Bhutan has always been self-sufficient as regards its food-consumption. Cattle products - butter, milk, cheese and meat - are a major part of the Bhutanese diet. The animals reared for food are bovines, pigs and poultry in southern Bhutan and the central valleys, and yaks in northern Bhutan, Bumthang and Mera Sakteng. Intense efforts are being made to increase productivity, veterinary farms have been set up and cross-breeding with imported animals has produced good results. Horses and mules are used exclusively as pack-animals and for riding, whilst sheep are raised for their wool, since traditionally their meat is eaten very little.

Two-thirds of Bhutan is covered by forests containing a wide variety of species (tropical trees, deciduous trees and conifers in the temperate zone), which constitute one of the country's most important potential sources of wealth. A policy of reafforestation and of scientifically controlled utilization of the forests is strictly applied by the Department of Forests which also created a school for foresters in 1971. A match factory, saw-mills and small private joinery businesses have been set up in agreement with the Department of Forests and this Department has itself established a factory for plywood, most of which is exported. In order to preserve the ecological balance of its environment, Bhutan has also created nine natural parks in which the fauna and flora are protected.

Mining resources were the object of prospecting in the period 1960-70 and amongst the minerals to be found under the ground in Bhutan are dolomite, coal, graphite, gypsum, marble, zinc, copper, lead, limestone and slate. Slate is now beginning to be worked and a cement plant, seventy percent of whose production is intended for export, was inaugurated in southern Bhutan in 1982. The other industries in Bhutan, apart from saw-mills and joinery, which are dependent on the products of the forest, are industries for processing agricultural products, such as canning factories and distilleries.

TWO CLOSELY RELATED SECTORS of economic activity are at present in a phase of rapid expansion: tourism and arts and crafts. Bhutan opened its doors to tourism in 1974. This industry is State operated and provides an important source of foreign exchange for the country. Individual tourism is very limited and almost all visitors must belong to a group. Their visit is organized by the governemental travel agency. In 1982-1983, the number of tourists to visit the country reached two thousand. The development of tourism has led to a boom in arts and crafts. This activity had in the past been entirely geared to producing for the home market but now has to adapt to different requirements. Traditional materials such as bamboo and wood are used to make items of furniture previously unknown in Bhutan, such as beds and lampshades. All the hotels in the country show their fidelity to traditional Bhutanese decorations, with a harmonious combination of Bhutanese and Western elements. Bhutanese arts and crafts are renowned for cloth woven on traditional looms, for bamboo, wood and precious metal work and for painted banners (thangkas) of religious inspiration. A painting school has been established so as to preserve traditional techniques of drawing and painting.

Economic development, however, involves improvements in the means of communication and in energy production. Bhutan has no railways and until February 1983 the only means of access to Bhutan was by road. This date marked the opening of a regular air link between Calcutta and Paro, which undoubtedly means the beginning of a new era for Bhutan, and a Paro-Dhaka route was opened in 1986.

Bhutan has a wide-ranging network of mule-tracks and bridges which remain the only means of access to many areas of the country. The road system has however expanded considerably since work started on the first road linking Phuntsholing to Thimphu and Paro in 1960. By 1986 there were some two thousand kilometres of roads, of which one thousand five hundred kilometres are metalled. Road-building has been hampered by a shortage of labour and workers have had to be recruited from abroad. Many bridges have also been built throughout the country to improve transport communications. The Government runs a public transport service, which has linked the different valleys since 1962, and a government-supervised service of privately-owned lorries provides for transport of goods.

A regular postal service began operating in 1962. The same year, Bhutan became a member of the Universal Postal Union. Bhutanese stamps are highly prized by collectors all over the world and the Government attaches great importance to their design and to their distribution. A telephone, telegraph and radio network links Bhutan to the outside world, as well as connecting different regions within the country. A radio station broadcasting in Dzongkha, Sharchopkha, Nepalese and English and a weekly paper in Dzongkha, Nepalese and English provide national and international news.

The large number of rivers, mountain streams and waterfalls gives Bhutan an enormous hydro-electric potential. Construction of small hydro-electric power stations has begun in the major urban centres. Diesel generators have also been installed since, although domestic energy requirements can be readily met with wood from the countryside, a quite understandable desire to have electricity is now being felt and the demand in urban centres has grown. A major Indo-Bhutanese hydro-electric project has been constructed in Chukha and this has started to supply about 330 megawatts in 1987. This amount of electricity will not only cover Bhutanese requirements but will make it possible to export electricity to India.

Economic development has also enabled Bhutan to transform its barter economy into a monetary economy. A currency has been established - the *Ngultrum* divided into a hundred *Chetrums* - and in 1968 the Bank of Bhutan was created. In 1982, the Royal Monetary Authority, whose role is that of a central bank, was inaugurated.

EDUCATION IS ONE OF THE MAIN CONCERNS of the Government, since the future of the country depends on its younger generations if Bhutan is to achieve its goal of self-reliance. Till the early 60's, there were virtually no modern educational facilities inside Bhutan, apart from the traditional education given in the monasteries. However it should be noted that some

Bhutanese received a formal education first in Haa valley and then abroad under the patronage of the previous Kings and of the late Prime Minister Jigme Dorje. Today, there are one hundred and fifty-two primary and secondary schools with thirty-six thousand pupils spread over the country. Most of the pupils are boarders with the schools providing their board and lodgings free of charge. A college equivalent to the first two years of university has also been set up and a fully-fledged university is being planned. Many students pursue advanced studies abroad, with scholarships from the Bhutanese Government, the UN or from the host-country. Great importance has been attached to the creation of technical colleges, which correspond to the most urgent needs of the country, and teacher-training establishments.

The teaching of Dzongkha, the official language, is being very actively promoted, but English is the medium of education so as to facilitate contact with the outside world. Students are given guidance in their choice of subjects by a government commission which subsequently provides them with jobs in the various branches of Government where their services are required.

FOR CENTURIES, the Bhutanese considered the illnesses from which they suffered to be the results of bad behaviour or of the influence of evil spirits. Oracles were consulted, followed by religious ceremonies, and this went hand in hand with treatment by medicinal plants, the use of which constituted a highly elaborate science. Today, centres for traditional medicine are being set up with the help of the World Health Organization. Parallel to the preservation of traditional medicine, one of the major projects of the Government since 1962 has been to establish modern medical facilities, available to all the Bhutanese right across the country.

Average life expectancy in Bhutan is 43, but the reason for which is the rate of infant mortality which is as high as one hundred forty seven per thousand. The mountainous nature of the country, which makes communications difficult, prevents the speedy development of natal and post-natal care. The most frequent illnesses are respiratory and gastro-intestinal, with a high incidence of goitres as a result of the lack of iodine in the traditional diet. Measles continues to ravage the child population.

Bhutan now has twelve hospitals, forty dispensaries and more than forty Basic Health Units, as well as three leprosy centres. Major campaigns for the control and elimination of malaria (in southern Bhutan), of tuberculosis (using BCG vaccinations), of goitres (by distributing iodized salt) and of leprosy are being carried out with the help of the WHO and UNICEF. Conditions of hygiene are far from perfect and the Governement is making efforts to inculcate basic notions of hygiene by organizing training sessions throughout the countryside.

Whilst the Bhutanese still perform ceremonies in the event of illness, they are reacting favourably to the introduction of new methods of treatment and the two "systems" are used together in many families to the advantage of all concerned.

H AS THIS INTRODUCTION, however schematically, achieved its goal? Has it managed to show all the different facets of Bhutan? Has it made it possible to understand how a rich past and centuries of tradition have combined with steady but restrained economic development and spectacular social progress over the last twenty years to make Bhutan one of the most astonishing and fascinating countries in the world? During these years, this country has experienced profound changes and undergone cultural shocks which might have created instability or destroyed Bhutan's awareness of its cultural heritage. None of this has in fact happened, since the Government has always endevoured to take account of the aspirations of the people and takes care never to offend against ancestral values. The monarchy, which in many countries is a conservative institution hampering change and progress, is in Bhutan a dynamic force which is instrumental in bringing about economic innovation and social progress.

Bhutan is neither a Shangri-La nor a poverty-stricken country. It does not fit into any of the stereotyped images of the "least-developed nations". With its small population, abundant material resources, and its fidelity to tradition, there is every reason to hope for a well-balanced future for these "Southern Valleys" hidden in the folds of the immense Himalayas.

1

Dzongs, monasteries, temples and chortens

BHUTAN IS FAMOUS for the quality of its architecture, which finds its most perfect expression in the dzongs, introduced into the country by the Shabdrung Ngawang Namgyel (1594-1651) in the 17th century. These monasteries and fortresses house both a state monastery and the administrative and judicial offices of each region. Each major valley has its dzong, which played an important strategic role in the past.

The dzongs are built as variants of a basic model: a quadrilateral of buildings enclosing one or more courtyards. A central tower called the *utse* often marks the division between the religious and the civil quarters, which are strictly separated. The wood carvings and paintings that decorate the dzongs are often outstandingly complex and subtle.

In addition to the dzongs, countless state-run or privately owned monasteries and temples are scattered throughout the country. They are often only distinguishable from large private houses by the red band on the wall and by the banner of victory, or *gyeltshen*, in gilded copper on the roof.

The chorten, or "receptacle of offerings", is a Buddhist monument whose origin lies in the "tumulus" *stupa* of ancient India. It is a votive monument to the memory of the Buddha or his meritorious deeds. Chortens soon came to be built to the memory of important religious figures, as well as to mark the victory of Buddhism over indigenous divinities. The symbolic significance of the chorten requires that the building consist of five parts, corresponding to the five elements of the cosmos, earth, water, fire, air and ether.

The architecture of the chorten developed regional variations: chortens in the Nepalese style have a large stepped base and a voluminous hemispherical structure, and eyes are painted on the cubelike upper part. The chorten of the High Himalayas and of the Tibetan plateau is lengthened and the hemispherical structure has taken the form of an inverted bell. In Bhutan, a superstructure is often built over the whole chorten, covering it totally, so that it resembles a small house.

1
Tashichho Dzong, Thimphu

2 Stairway of the central tower, Tashichho Dzong

3 Interior courtyard, Tashichho Dzong

4   Taktsang

5 Taktsang

6 Punakha Dzong

7 Paro Dzong and bridge

8 Paro Dzong and paddy fields

9   Kuje Lhakhang, in Bumthang

10   Drugyel Dzong

11 Dungtse Lhakhang

12 Tongsa Dzong

13 Tongsa Dzong

14   Wangdiphodrang Dzong

15 Interior courtyard, Wangdiphodrang

16   Tachogang

17   Dechenphug

18 Gom Kora

19 Tashigang Dzong

20 Chendebji Chorten

21 Chorten Kora

2|3

Tashichho Dzong, Thimphu

The "Fortress of the Auspicious Religion" (Tashichho Dzong) is the finest example of the architecture of the Thimphu valley. The original dzong is said to have been built here by a monk of the Lhapa order in the late 12th century. The fortress was offered in 1641 to the Shabdrung Ngawang Namgyel, who gave it its present name. The dzong burnt down in the 18th century, and was rebuilt on the present site. When the third king of Bhutan, Jigme Dorji Wangchuck (1928-1972) chose Thimphu as his permanent capital, he decided to make the dzong the headquarters of the central government. Extensive reconstruction was undertaken in 1962 and finished in 1969. Besides its function as seat of government, the dzong is now also the central state monastery, and houses the National Assembly Hall where deputies assemble twice a year.

Photograph No. 2 shows the stairway of the central tower, which, like all stairways in Bhutan, is exceedingly steep, and No. 3 the courtyard in the religious quarters of the dzong.

4|5

Taktsang

The Bhutanese consider Taktsang a holy place and pilgrims reach it on foot after several hours' climb through an eerie forest whose massive trees are festooned with lichen. The monastery is perched on a rocky bluff in the Paro valley overlooking a vertiginous drop of 1,000 metres. The site is particulary venerated because of its associations with Guru Rinpoche, who is said to have arrived here in his form of Dorje Droloe, mounted on a flying tiger. The name Taktsang means "tiger's den".

The present monastery is made up of numerous buildings of different dates, but its most important founder was the 4th Desi, Tenzin Rabgye (1638-1696), who built the principal temple in 1692. The legend is that after having prayed to Guru Rinpoche, he cut off his hair and threw it into the abyss. Rocks miraculously sprang up upon the Desi's hair, and these served as the underpinnings of the temple.

6

Punakha Dzong

This gigantic dzong is built on a tongue of land at the confluence of the rivers Pho and Mo, in the valley of Punakha which is famous for its mild climate and its tropical fruits. The fortress was established in 1637 by the Shabdrung Ngawang Namgyel and was repeatedly rebuilt after a series of fires. Until the 1950's, it was the winter capital of Bhutan, but it is still lively in the winter months when monks of the central state monastery come here to escape the relatively severe climate of Thimphu.

7|8

Paro Dzong

The white mass of this dzong overlooks the fertile valley of Paro. It appears that in the 15th century a small dzong existed here, which was given to the Shabdrung Ngawang Namgyel in 1645. The new dzong built by the Shabdrung was accidentally destroyed by fire in 1907 but was immediately rebuilt by the Penlop, or governor, of Paro, Dawo Penjor. Today it is both a state monastery and the administrative seat of the district of Paro. Like most dzongs, its function was strategic and it is approached by a covered bridge. The dzong itself was protected by the watch tower, or *ta dzong*, that can be seen on the upper right hand corner of the photograph No. 7. This building now houses the National Museum and contains innumerable treasures of Bhutanese arts and crafts.

9

Kuje Lhakhang, in Bumthang

Bumthang is one of Bhutan's most historically important regions. Made up of four valleys, it has numerous temples and monasteries, many of which have great importance in the history of the country. Kuje which means "the impression of Guru Rinpoche's body" is particularly cherished since it was blessed by the presence of Guru Rinpoche in the second half of the 8th century A.D. earlier to his visit to Tibet. Three buildings now stand at the place where he meditated to discover the "vital principle" of the legendary king Sentha. The building on the right was built in 1652 by Migyur Tenpa, the 3rd Desi of Bhutan, while the building to the left was built in 1900 by Ugyen Wangchuck, the governor of Tongsa, or Tongsa Penlop, at that time before he became the first king. Kuje houses the largest statue of Guru Rinpoche in Bhutan. A third building is now being constructed under the patronage of H.M. the Queen Mother of Bhutan.

10

Drugyel Dzong

This dzong, at the north-west extremity of the Paro valley, was built in 1647 by the Shabdrung Ngawang Namgyel to commemorate his victory over the Tibetan army. Hence its name, which means "Dzong of victorious Drukpa". It was destroyed in 1951 by a fire started by a butter lamp and is now a solitary ruin.
On clear days, the white peak of Mt. Jomolhari (7,314 metres high) stands out behind its ramparts.

11

Dungtse Lhakhang

Dungtse Lhakhang is a temple, unusual in that its shape resembles a chorten. Tradition says that it was built in the 15th century by the saint Thangtong Gyelpo (1385-1464) to subjugate the divinity, a serpent or a tortoise, that lived under the mountain at whose foot the temple stands. The temple is decorated with numerous paintings, probably executed in the first half of the 19th century under the orders of the 25th religious leader of Bhutan, Sherab Gyeltshen (1772-1848), who had the building restored.

12|13

Tongsa Dzong

Tongsa, which is laid out on several levels, is probably the biggest and most impressive dzong in Bhutan. Situated in the heart of the country, it is perched on a ridge that is separated from the mountain range and dominates a narrow valley. From the dzong, the view over the gorge formed by the River Mangde is breath-taking and, by virtue of its strategic position, the dzong governs the roads leading from west to east and from north to south. In the past, the mule path went through the dzong itself, so that no one could cross the valley without the knowledge of the chief of the dzong. The original fortress was built in 1543 by the great-grandfather of the Shabdrung, Ngagi Wangchuck (1517-1554). In the middle of the 17th century, the governor of Tongsa, who was to become the 3rd Desi of Bhutan, Migyur Tenpa (1613-1680), enlarged the dzong and important restoration was carried out after the earthquake of 1897. Before the establishment of the monarchy, the Tongsa Penlop was one of the most powerful men in Bhutan. Ugyen Wangchuck (1862-1926), who became the first king of Bhutan in 1907, held the title, and it is now customary for the crown prince to assume the title of Tongsa Penlop.

47

14|15

Wangdiphodrang Dzong

The fortress of Wangdiphodrang stands like a figurehead on the crest of a rocky spur. Built in 1638 by the Shabdrung Ngawang Namgyel, it keeps watch in this windswept valley over the highway to eastern Bhutan. The particular charm of the dzong lies in its roof of silvered shingles, held in place in the traditional manner by heavy stones (photo No. 14) and to its narrow courtyards, with their long balconies (photo No. 15). The chapel of the fearsome divinity, often hidden from sight, is clearly indicated here by the black windows, painted with gesticulating skeletons and grinning masks.

16

Tachogang

This splendid temple is framed by the arid setting of the entrance to the Paro valley. It was founded in the 15th century by the saint Thangtong Gyelpo, to commemorate the vision he is said to have had here of Avalokiteshvara in his form of Balaha ("excellent horse") who is known as Tacho in Dzongkha, hence the name of the temple.

The temple, on the left bank of the Paro Chu, was linked to the other side by one of the celebrated iron-chain bridges constructed by the saint.

17

Dechenphug

This monastery is located in a charming little inlet in the upper Thimphu valley. Its tall red tower indicates that it is the residence of the guardian divinity of the valley, Jagpa Melen, who was subjugered and immured in a rock by the Drukpa monk Kunga Senge (1314-1347).

18

Gom Kora

The temple of Gom Kora is situated on an alluvial terrace at an altitude of 800 metres, 25 kilometres north of Tashigang. Surrounded by paddy fields and banana groves, it is a holy place where Guru Rinpoche is said to have meditated. A huge black rock near the temple is supposed to be the place where Guru Rinpoche went into retreat, emerging later in the shape of a mythical bird, the "jachung", or "garuda". The rock has two entrances, and legend says that

virtuous people can enter on one side and come out on the other, while sinners can find no way out.

19

Tashigang Dzong

Founded around 1656, Tashigang is the country's easternmost dzong. It is the administrative seat of the eastern district, and is situated in a remarkable strategic position at the summit of a rocky bluff overlocking the arid gorge of the Dangme Chu River.

20

Chendebji Chorten

This unusually large chorten is situated at
the bottom of a wild valley on the road
between the Pele-la Pass and Tongsa. It was
built by a monk named Shida in the first
half of the 18th century to appease the valley's powerful guardian spirit. The architectural style closely resembles that of Nepalese
chortens.

21

Chorten Kora

In the region of Tashiyangtse, north of
Tashigang, a wide valley with paddy fields
opens up at the end of a gorge covered
with luxurious vegetation. In the middle of
the fields stands the gigantic Chorten Kora,
built, like Chendebji Chorten, in the Nepalese style. The exact date of its foundation
is unknown, though it is said to have been
renovated during the reign of the 2nd king
Jigme Wangchuck (1905-1952). Legend has it
that a Bhutanese brought the model for
it to Bhutan sculpted in a turnip.

2

Religious art

22 Wheel of Life, Chorten Kora

23   Cosmic mandala, Paro Dzong

24 Cosmic mandala, Simtokha Dzong

25 Cosmic mandala, Paro Dzong

26 Cosmic mandala, Paro Dzong

27 The Buddha and the 16 arhats, National Museum

28 The White Tara, National Museum

29 Episode from the life of Guru Rinpoche, Tango monastery

30
Phajo Drugom Shigpo,
Tango monastery

31 The Shabdrung Ngawang Namgyel, National Museum

32 Thangtong Gyelpo, Simtokha Dzong

33   The great coronation *thangka* of H.M. King Jigme Singye Wangchuck

34 A *Tashigomang*, a portable shrine

35   An altar, Gangtey monastery

36 Yonten Gyeltshen, Phajoding monastery

37 *Tormas*, ritual cakes

38 Prayer wheels, Simtokha Dzong

22

Wheel of Life
(Mural painting, Chorten Kora,
eastern Bhutan)
This "Wheel of Life" painting, traditionally
shown at the entrance of temples and
monasteries, represents the six (sometimes
five) realms of existence in the chain of
reincarnation. In the centre are the three
principal factors responsible for reincarnations in the different realms. The pig
symbolizes ignorance, the snake anger and
the cock desire. The circle broken into two
halves, one black, the other white, symbolizes the path that leads to good and bad
reincarnations. In the upper part of the
wheel are the three favourable domains,
which are, from left to right, those of the
titans, or demigods, of the gods and of
the human beings. In the lower part are
the three unfavourable domains, of the *pre-
tas*, or hungry ghosts, of the hells and of
the animals.
The painting is altogether unusual, because
of its irregular shape, which only distantly
resembles the traditional wheel. Even more
so are the four white pointed shapes that
appear at the top and bottom of the painting, which suggest fangs or tusks, and are
probably a transposition of the fangs, feet
and hands between which Mara, the god of
existence, usually holds the wheel of reincarnations.

23 | 24
25 | 26

Cosmic mandalas
(Mural paintings, Paro Dzong and
Simtokha Dzong)
These four mural paintings, from Paro
Dzong (Nos. 23, 25 and 26) and Simtokha
Dzong (No. 24) are all representations of
Buddhist cosmology.
The first group (Nos. 23 and 24) represents
the classical Buddhist cosmology, whose
most systematic and authentic exposition is
to be found in the *Abhidharmakosha*, written in the 5th century by an Indian scholar
named Vasubandhu. In the centre is
Mt. Sumeru, the central pillar of the
cosmos and home of various gods.
Mt. Sumeru is surrounded by seven ranges
of golden mountains.
In the Paro Dzong painting (No. 23), the
four continents lie outside these ranges on
the four compass points. They have different forms (the northern continent is hidden by Mt. Sumeru), and each is composed
of a principal continent and two subsidiary
ones. It is in the southern continent,
Jambudvipa, shown at the bottom of the painting, that we live. The exterior circle closes
this representation of the Buddhist cosmos.

In the painting from Simtokha Dzong
(No. 24), the mountain ranges are symbolized by yellow concentric squares, but the
four continents do not appear. The circles
in different colours represent the 12 months
of the year. The path of the sun during the
year is shown by an ellipsoidal line in brick
red. The sun follows its trajectory, passing
from one circle to the next, and the period
between two new moons, during which it
crosses a circle, is shown by a thicker por-
tion of coloured line.
The second group (Nos. 25 and 26) represents the cosmology as explained in the
Kalacakra-tantra, "The Wheel of Time", one
of the principal texts of Tantric Buddhism
(ca. 10th century). Painting No. 25 represents the cosmos seen from above, divided
into four wide concentric circles
of different colours. Each represents one of
the four elements: air (yellow, on the outside), fire (red), water (light blue) and earth
(dark blue). On the circle of the earth the
continents of the four compass points are
laid out in a different way from that of the
Abhidharmakosha. Inside the circle of
the earth are 18 small circles in bright
colours, which represent the combination
of continent-ocean-mountain six times
(6 x 3 = 18). The central part, divided into
five portions, is Mt. Sumeru, which is
shown in elevation in painting No. 26.
Here, the circle of the earth is not shown
and the four continents are placed on the
circle of water which is unusual.
In painting No. 25, the 12 large thin circles
of bright colours represented on the circles
of water and earth are identical to those of
the Abhidharmakosha (cf. photo No. 24)
and represent the 12 months.

27

The Buddha and the 16 arhats

(Thangka, National Museum, Paro)

The thangka is one of the most characteristic forms of Bhutanese art. It is a scroll, generally painted on cotton cloth and framed by bands of brocade.

In the centre of this thangka, the Buddha Shakyamuni is seated in the classical posture of meditation, making the gesture of taking the earth as witness. Slightly below, and on each side of his lotus throne, are his two principle disciples, Maudgalyayana and Shariputra, wearing monk's robes and making gestures of offering. In front of the Buddha's throne is a small low table, on either side of which are represented Hashang, a Chinese saint, extremely popular on account of his rounded belly, and Dharmatala, accompanied by a tiger. These last two personages were added to the classical list of the 16 arhats, bringing their number to 18. The 16 arhats, guardians of Buddhism in different parts of the universe, frame the Buddha in setting of rocks and foliage. In the upper part of the thangka are two medallions, one containing the green Tara and the other the Buddha Amitabha. In the lower corners, in the middle of swirling clouds and flames, are the four Great Kings of the orients.

28

The White Tara

(Thangka, National Museum, Paro)

Tantric Buddhism has numerous divinities, both male and female, peaceful and fearsome, which, to the uninitiated, may seem a complex and impenetrable pantheon. In fact, these divinities are classified into several distinct families, a system that this thangka illustrates well.

At the top of the painting is the red Buddha Amitabha, head of the Padma, or lotus, family. On his right is seated one of the best-known bodhisattvas of this line, Avalokiteshvara, in white, with four arms. On the left stands the goddess Tara in her green form. The principal figure also represents the goddess, but in her white form. The green and the white Tara are both female manifestations of the bodhisattva Avalokiteshvara. According to tradition, they were born from the tears that Avalokiteshvara, the compassionate, shed for the sins of men.

29

Episode from the life of Guru Rinpoche

(Mural painting, Tango monastery, Thimphu valley)

The life of Guru Rinpoche is the source of an extremely popular literary cycle, also represented pictorially in a very vivid style. This scene represents the episode during which Guru Rinpoche was adopted as crown prince by Indrabhuti, king of the land of Uddiyana.

30

Phajo Drugom Shigpo

(Mural painting, Tango monastery, Thimphu valley)

The principal personage of this painting, clothed in rich brocade, is Phajo Drugom Shigpo (1184-1211), a holy man who introduced the Middle Drukpa order (Bar-Druk) to western Bhutan. He founded several monasteries and temples, one of which was the monastery of Tango in the upper Thimphu valley, where this mural painting is situated. He married a woman from the Thimphu valley, Sonam Peldren, who is seen here kneeling in a gesture of offering. The four figures playing below are their four sons, who where sent into the different regions and continued to spread their father's religious teachings. In the 17th century, when the Shabdrung Ngawang Namgyel arrived in Bhutan from Tibet, it was their descendants who welcomed him and helped him to establish the hegemony of the Drukpa order.

31

The Shabdrung Ngawang Namgyel
(Thangka, National Museum, Paro)
This thangka represents the Shabdrung Ngawang Namgyel, a monk of the Drukpa Kagyupa school who unified Bhutan in the 17th century. The figures surrounding him are, starting from the top left: the Tibetan king Khrisong Detsen (8th century), Ngagi Wangchuck, a form of Avalokiteshvara, Tshepame (Amitayus), the Tibetan king Songtseng Gampo (7th century), the Indian master Shantarakshita, who travelled to Tibet during the reign of Khrisong Detsen. In the second row, Naropa, a 10th-century Indian master who exercised a dominant influence on the Kagyupa school, Gampopa (1079-1153), a Tibetan master of the Kagyupa school. In the 3rd row, Tsangpa Gyare (1161-1211), a Tibetan master who founded the Drukpa Kagyupa school, and Pema Karpo, king of

the northern land of Shambhala and the great scholar of the Drukpa school, who bore the same name, is considered to have been his reincarnation. In the 4th row, the *umdze* (leader of the religious ceremonies) Tenzin Drugyel (1591-1656) and Damchoe Pekar Jungne (1604-1672), the two principal disciples of the Shabdrung, who were to become respectively the first Desi, temporal ruler of Bhutan, and the first Je Khenpo, the religious head. In the last row are Jampel Dorji (1631-1681), son of the Shabdrung, Tsuglag Gyamtsho (18th century), reincarnation of Sangnag Gyamtsho, and Tsewang Tenzin (1574-1643), incarnation of Phajo Drugom Shigpo (cf. photo 30) and father of Tenzin Rabgye, the 4th Desi of Bhutan.

32

Thangtong Gyelpo
(Carved slate, Simtokha Dzong)
This half-naked figure, wrapped in a flowing cloak, his hair caught up into a strange hairstyle, is the *Drupthob* ("Accomplished") Thangtong Gyelpo (1385-1464). He is renowned for having built the first iron bridges in the country, which earned him the name of Chaksampa, "he who makes the iron bridges", and he is always represented with an iron chain in his right hand. The nectar vase that he holds in his lap symbolizes one of the cycles of religious teachings, the Tshebum, or "vase of longevity".

33

The great coronation *thangka*
A large thangka like this one, used for festivals, is called a *thondrol*, which means "whose very sight brings liberation" (from the cycle of transmigratory existence). The central figure represents Guru Rinpoche, whom the Nyingmapa order, which he founded, consider to be the Second Buddha. Above him is the red Buddha Amitabha. The eight other forms of Guru

Rinpoche are set out in two vertical ranks on the two sides of the thangka. On the left are, from top to bottom, the Guru in his forms Tshokye Dorje, Shakya Sengye, Loden Cokse and Senge Dradro. On the right, from top to bottom, are Pema Gyelpo, Padmasambhava, Nyima Oezer and Dorje Droloe. On the right and left of the head of the central figure are the bodhisattva Avalokiteshvara and the divinity Usnisa-vijaya.

The two female figures to the right and left of Guru Rinpoche are his two consorts, Mandarawa and Yeshe Tshogyel. Below the throne are two religious personages: the Shabdrung Ngawang Namgyel (to the right of Guru Rinpoche) and Pema Lingpa (1450-1521).

This appliqué thangka was mainly commissioned for the Kuje temple in Bumthang. Its completion coincided with the auspicious installation of present King Jigme Singye Wangchuck as Tongsa Penlop and it was displayed on the occasion of his Coronation which took place in 1974 in Tashichho Dzong in Thimphu. The consecration ceremony of the *thondrol* was conducted three times by His Holiness the Je Khenpo, Lam Sonam Zangpo and Dilgo Khentse Rinpoche. Further His Holiness the Dilgo Khentse Rinpoche blessed it by adding some of the Buddha's relics to it. It is now kept in the Kuje temple in Bumthang.

34

A *tashigomang,* a portable shrine

The *tashigomang,* or "auspicious shrine with numerous doors" is a portable shrine that the *manip,* "who chants the prayers", transports on his back from one village to the next. As its name indicates, the tashigomang is a structure with many doors, large and small, that the manip opens and shuts. This shrine contains numerous statues and paintings of the Buddha, bodhisattvas and monks.

There are several types of tashigomang. The one photographed here represents the Zangdo Pelri, or "glorious copper-coloured mountain", the palace of Guru Rinpoche, another name for whom is Padmasambhava, the founder of the "ancient" Nyingmapa order. The statue of Guru Rinpoche sitting on a lotus flower at the top of this structure symbolizes the miraculous birth of the saint in a lotus flower on Lake Danakosha in the land of Uddiyana.

The introduction of the tashigomang to Bhutan is attributed to the Shabdrung Ngawang Namgyel, who sent manips, each carrying a tashigomang, into each of the provinces of Bhutan to propagate Buddhism among the people. The manip who chants the prayers beside the tashigomang is considered a religious person, but may marry and in many respects live the life of a lay person.

35

An altar from the monastery of Gangtey

This richly decorated altar is to be found in the monastery of Gangtey, one of the most important religious establishments of western Bhutan. It is the seat of an important line of incarnations of Pema Thrinle, grandson of the great Nyingmapa saint Pema Lingpa (1450-1521). The wealth of the monastery is evident in the decoration and in particular in the profusion of colours and gold. The tripartite division of the principal sanctum, in front of which the offerings table is placed, is typical of a Bhutanese temple. The principal object of veneration here is the commemorative chorten of one of the incarnations of the monastery of Gangtey. It is flanked on the left by the Buddha Shakyamuni and on the right by Guru Rinpoche.

36

Yonten Gyeltshen
(Statue, Phajoding monastery,
Thimphu valley)
This statue, notable for its sculptural
beauty, is that of Yonten Gyeltshen
(1804-1870), who occupied the post of
31st Je Khenpo, head of the religious establishment of Bhutan, from 1851 to 1858.

 37

Ritual cakes *(tormas)*
The *torma* is a ritual cake used in all religious ceremonies in Bhutan. Made from a
mixture of butter and flour, it is given different forms and colours depending on the
divinities for which is it intended. For less
important ceremonies it may be very
simple, but for a grandiose ceremony it
becomes extremely elaborate, like the one
pictured here.

 38

Prayer wheels
(Simtokha Dzong)
Prayer wheels are a well-established religious
tradition in Bhutan. Inside each cylinder
are rolled long sheets of paper on which the
same prayer is written thousands of times.
Then passers-by turn the wheels, always in
a clockwise direction, the prayer wheels
"recite" a single prayer thousands of times.
This act wins merit, and helps to obtain a
good reincarnation.
The prayer wheels shown here are inserted
into the niches that surround the central
tower of Simtokha Dzong, at the entrance
to the Thimphu valley. The cylinders are
inscribed with sacred formulae in an orna-
mental script called *lantsa*. The base of
each of the niches is decorated with the
magnificent carved slates that are one of
the highest achievements of Bhutanese art,
and which represent different divinities,
saints and great monks (cf. picture No. 32).
The openings of these wooden niches, painted with flowers and jewels, take up the traditional architectural motifs that frame
Bhutanese windows.

3

Monastic life

IN THE PAST, almost every family sent at least one of its sons to one of the numerous monasteries scattered all over the country, and monks made up a considerable percentage of the male population. Today, the situation has changed considerably, but there are still very many monks, who play an important part in the everyday life of the nation.

Boys are admitted to the monasteries at an early age (5 or 6 years old) and are placed under the tutorship of a master, an older and educated monk. A boy who is recognized as an incarnation may begin his monastic life at 3 or 4 years old.

The monks follow a discipline set down in the canon and live regular life, observing monastic vows, whose number varies according to their status: postulant, novice or fully ordained monk. The young monks first learn to read and write, but in addition take part in various ceremonies.

The religious literature is incredibly rich and extensive, and includes, amongst other texts, the Kanjur (Collection of the Words of the Buddha) and the Tenjur (Collection of Commentaries on the Kanjur), as well as the complete works of eminent masters, and treatises on philosophy, medicine, astrology and so on. Under the guidance of their master, young monks learn numerous texts by heart. The rites of Bhutanese Buddhism are extremely elaborate. The recitation of rituals is accompanied by several musical instruments, such as the shawm, cymbals, drums and so on. The altars are richly decorated with butter lamps, brightly coloured ritual cakes and other objects (see pictures 35 and 37).

Although the monks perform daily, monthly and annual rituals in the monasteries as well as pursuing their studies, they are not confined to the monastery itself. They may be asked to visit families to perform rituals. On occasions such as the birth of a child, weddings or deaths, monks are called in to perform the appropriate rites. Some especially religious families who are wealthy enough may house one or more monks for varying lengths of time, so that they can perform rituals to protect the household and help it to acquire merit.

It must be added that in Bhutan monks of the Drukpa monasteries take the vow of celibacy. Certain monks of the Nyingmapa order, on the other hand, are not bound by this vow and may marry.

A special category of religious persons, called *Gomchen*, is found, particularly in eastern Bhutan. Their status lies somewhere between that of the layman, since they are peasants and lead a family life, and that of the monk, since on certain occasions they perform rituals in the temples and in the homes of private citizens.

In 1986, for the first time, some forty young men who had completed secondary school entered monasteries at their own request. This event undoubtedly symbolizes a new dynamism in the clergy.

40 Lopon Nyapchi

41 A thirsty young monk

42   Monks at the Thimphu *Tshechu*

43   Young monk watching at the Thimphu *Tshechu*

44 Lopon Khandro at Simtokha Dzong
Young monks studying 45

39

A ritual

Countless and highly varied rituals take place in all Bhutanese households and the number of monks depends to a large extent on the wealth of the householder. As the incense smokes, the monks, seated by order of precedence, chant sacred texts, punctuating their recitation with short pieces of music and with symbolic hand movements.

40|41

Lopon Nyapchi   A thirsty young monk

The term *Lopon* before this monk's name is an honorary title for high-ranking monks which means "master". But this same term of *Lopon* is also used as a respectful form of address for all laymen from the rank of clerk upwards.

In exchange for the education they receive, young monks must perform small tasks for their master: fetching water, lighting fires and sweeping rooms. Such tasks are carried out by the novices, like other children, with varying amounts of enthusiasm!

42

Monks at the Thimphu *Tshechu*

The monks consider the annual festival of the tshechu, in their monastery as one of the most important events of the year, and eagerly look forward to it. Some of them also take part as dancers and musicians.

43

Young monk watching the Thimphu *Tshechu*

The fascination of the events that are taking place is evident in the face of this young monk, who has found an observation post tailored to fit him.

44

Lopon Khandro at Simtokha Dzong

Lopon Khandro is one of the masters who teaches at Simtokha Dzong. This dzong, built in 1629, was transformed by the late king Jigme Dorji Wangchuck into a college for training teachers of the national language Dzongkha. Also the traditional texts are taught here as well as calligraphy, the engraving of texts on wood and woodblock printing, the traditional Bhutanese method of printing. The students are laymen, but work under the direction of monks.

45

Young monks studying

Young monks spend a part of their day learning by heart the texts that their master teaches them. They sway backwards and forwards as they chant these difficult texts at the top of their voices, though their deeper meaning may elude them for some time.

4
Landscapes

46 Forest scene with pink rhododendrons

47   Aerial view of a fluvial valley in Bhutan

48 The Paro valley and the palace of Ugyen Pelri

Paddy fields in the Paro valley

50 Fields in the Radi valley

51 A farm at Radi

52   The old bridge at Tashiyangtse

53 Water-driven prayer wheel in the Choekhor valley of Bumthang

54 Prayer wall near the Kuje temple

55   The Choekhor valley of Bumthang and the Kuje temple

56 Prayer flags and wall in the Choekhor valley

57
Prayer flags near Simtokha Dzong

58 Pass above Phajoding

59 Yak

60   Yaks near the Pele-la pass

61 Spanish moss-covered tree

46

Forest scene with pink rhododendrons

The rhododendron is the national flower of Bhutan and there are several hundred varieties, some of which may attain a height of many feet. They flower from the beginning of April to the end of May, depending on the altitude (between approximately 2,000 and 4,000 metres) with colours ranging from golden yellow and white through all the shades of pink and red. The splash of colour of a rhododendron bush in the forest is always a visual delight.

47

Aerial view of a fluvial valley in Bhutan

48

The Paro valley and the palace of Ugyen Pelri

Below Paro Dzong is the palace of Ugyen Pelri, one of the residences of the royal family. It was built by the Paro Penlop, Tshering Penjor around 1930 on the model of Zangdo Pelri, the celestial palace of Ugyen Guru Rinpoche, hence its name Ugyen Pelri. Behind the palace is the temple of Druk Choeding, built by Ngawang Choegyel (1465-1540), an ancestor of the Shabdrung Ngawang Namgyel. The temple marks the entrance to the little bazaar of Paro.

49

Paddy fields in the Paro valley

The valley of Paro is one of Bhutan's main rice-producing areas, and its population enjoy a better standard of living than in most other parts of the country. This photo shows the paddy fields of Paro in an unusual light: it is October, the harvest is almost completed, as one can see from the sheaves of rice lying in the fields, and the

monsoon is long since over. However, the unseasonable early snowfalls of 1982 give the scene an uncharacteristic watery look.

50

Fields in the Radi valley

Radi is a fertile valley situated to the east of Tashigang. Rice, maize and banana trees grow easily here, thanks to its almost tropical climate. As is common in Bhutan, the cattle are brought to graze in the fields after the grain has been cut.

51

A farm at Radi

The farms of the Radi valley are, as is common in the rest of Bhutan, situated in the middle of their fields, which means that dwellings are scattered over a large area. They are made of stone and covered with shingles, and are typical of the Bhutanese houses. In October, the roofs are covered in flaming red, this being the season when the Bhutanese dry the large chilli peppers. These are one of the staples of the Bhutanese diet, rather than simply a spice, as in the West.

52

The old bridge at Tashiyangtse

Tashiyangtse is a dzong situated in dense forest north of Tashigang in eastern Bhutan. To reach it, one has to cross this bridge, which is built according to the traditional balanced cantilever principle. The roof and sides are made of woven bamboo, typical of eastern Bhutan. In western Bhutan, the same type of bridge is roofed with wood shingles.

53

Water-driven prayer-wheel in the Choekhor valley of Bumthang

Throughout the countryside of Bhutan, it is common to see these small buildings built over streams, and to hear the clanging of their bells. They contain a large prayer wheel driven by water, which, as it turns, strikes the bell with a small stick attached to its upper edge.

54

Prayer wall near the Kuje temple

Prayer walls are a part of the Bhutanese landscape, a manifestation of the fervour of the people. They can be made of bare stones or of stones that are painted and engraved with the sacred formulae of the three protectors of Tantric Buddhism: Avalokiteshvara (Chenrezi), Vajrapani (Chagna Dorji) and Manjushri (Jampeyang). The most frequently engraved inscription, however, is that of Avalokiteshvara, "Om mani padme hum".

55

The Choekhor valley of Bumthang and the Kuje temple

Bumthang is a complex of four valleys, the largest of which, Choekhor, is the widest in all Bhutan. The fields, where barley, buckwheat and wheat are the principal crops, are enclosed by woven bamboo fences. The temple of Kuje, seen beyond the fields (and shown in greater details in photo No. 9) is situated to the north of the valley.

56

Prayer flags and wall in the Choekhor valley

Certain prayer walls are not as elaborate as those shown in photograph 54 and are simply heaps of stones, of which only the uppermost are inscribed. The prayer flags, which are also manifestations of Buddhist faith, are set up near holy places and in dangerous places like mountain passes, bridges and so on, that might be inhabited by demons. They are also set up for the benefit of the dead. The flags carry holy inscriptions in woodblock print and the wind carries these off to the gods.

57

Prayer flags near Simtokha Dzong

These flags flap in the wind near Simtokha Dzong which guards the entrance to the Thimphu valley and the road that leads to the Dochu-la pass and to the valley of Punakha beyond.

58

Pass above Phajoding
This pass which looks out over the valley of Thimphu from an altitude of 4,000 metres is marked, like most passes, by prayer flags and a chorten. In the background are the snow-capped peaks of the Black Mountains range.

59

Yak
The scientific name of the yak, *bos grunniens*, is derived from its characteristic grunt, which resembles that of the bison and is not at all like the lowing of a cow. Despite its temperamental nature, the yak is a great provider for the nomads who live at altitudes of over 3,000 metres: yak hair is used to weave their black tents, rope and clothes. Its flesh is eaten and exchanged for rice, and the milk of the female (*dri*) is used to make highly valued butter and cheese. The yak is a very sure-footed animal and can cover long distances at great speed. Despite its indocility, it is used both as a pack animal and a mount and is even employed to plough the small plots of land cultivated by the nomads. Its dung is used as a valuable fuel.

60

Yaks near the Pele-la pass
The Pele-la pass lies at an altitude of 3,300 metres. It is an unusually open place covered with high altitude bamboos. Its gentle slopes are favourite pastures for the many yaks belonging to the nomads of the Black Mountains, which come down to spend the winter at this relatively low altitude. The number of yaks in Bhutan is estimated to be over 26,000.

61

Spanish moss-covered tree
This tree, and the Spanish moss that gives it such an unearthly apperance, is found in the forest that surrounds the monastery of Taktsang (photos Nos. 4 and 5) in the valley of Paro at altitudes of around 3,000 metres.

5

The valley of Sakteng

SAKTENG IS AN ISOLATED VALLEY east of Tashigang Dzong at an altitude of 3,000 metres. The inhabitants are different from those in the rest of Bhutan, and akin to the Monpa peoples of the region of Tawang in Arunachal Pradesh in India. Of Mongoloid stock, they speak a language of the Tibeto-Burmese family. Not much is yet known of these semi-nomad herdsmen *(Brokpas)*, also called *Dakpas*, a name which is shortened to *Daps* in the west. They live in austere drystone houses covered with shingles and grouped in villages surrounded with fields of corn, barley and beet. When springtime comes, they leave for the mountain pastures with their troops of yaks and crossbreeds of yaks, but on the way they also trade with their "cousins" on the other side of the frontier. During the winter months, some venture as far as the west of Bhutan, where they sell a highly prized butter and wooden vessels made only by them.

62   Caravan arriving at Sakteng

63 Sakteng at dawn

64 The valley and village of Sakteng

65 Typical house in Sakteng

66 People of Sakteng

67 Man of Sakteng

68 A villager and his horse

69 Diminutive shepherd

70   Man spinning wool

71 Weaver

72   A Sakteng dance

73 A Sakteng dance

62

Caravan arriving at Sakteng
These horsemen are entering the valley of
Sakteng. In the remotest areas of Bhutan,
the horse is the only mean of transport,
which lends an extra dimension to any trip.

63

Sakteng at dawn
The people of Sakteng are extremely religious and light small fires of juniper each
morning at dawn. The fragrant and
purifying smoke rises like an offering to
the gods.

64

The valley and village of Sakteng
From the pass that is indicated by the
"horses of the wind", the little white prayer
flags, the visitor comes upon the sizeable
village of Sakteng, whose houses crowd closely together. At the bottom of the valley
meanders the river that serves the whole
Sakteng region.

65

Typical house in Sakteng
Houses in the Sakteng valley have the typical features of Bhutanese architecture: small
juxtaposed windows, wooden famework.
These houses, however, give something of
an impression of austerity which perhaps
comes from the absence of those paintings
which generally embellish and enliven the
houses in the lower valleys.

66

People of Sakteng
The costume of the *Dakpas* is very different
from that of the Bhutanese. The women,
whoses hair is long, traditionally wear a
kind of red and white silk poncho with the
edges sewn together (the *shinka*), a red silk
jacket with long sleeves decorated with animal designs (the *totun*) and a red wool cape
(the *hemta*). Some wear a braided black
wool jacket. The men wear the *pishup*, trou-
sers of leather or cloth, over which are
worn ample flapped breeches in white wool
(the *kandam*), a roomy jacket of red wool
(the *chuba*) and a chasuble of leather (the
paktsa).
Rubber boots are coming to replace the traditional boots of leather and felt, the *lham*,
but the hat, or *gamashamo*, which is characteristic of the *Dakpas*, has no equivalent.
It is a flat bonnet in waterproof felt made
of yak hair, which has five descending
appendages that drain off the rain without
letting the head get wet. A felt disc, the
denthan, is also sometimes hung from the
belt and serves as a seat.

67

Man of Sakteng

The *Dakpas* are reputed for their somewhat wild beauty, which this man illustrates perfectly.

68

A villager and his horse

This man is captivated by his own likeness, which has just emerged from a polaroid camera. Photos like this are one of the best possible gifts in a region where photography is still unknown. The horse is covered with a saddle carpet of Tibetan origin. The Bhutanese do not traditionnally make carpets.

69

Diminutive shepherd

The *Dakpas* also breed sheep. This small shepherd, wearing traditional dress, already has the calm and untamed look of his elders.

70

Man spinning wool

Both men and women wear beautiful earrings decorated with turquoises. This man is spinning wool with a spindle. In some parts of the Himalayas, both men and women do the spinning.

71

Weaver

This girl is weaving wool on a frame loom with four pedals, which makes for a regular weave. Animal and geometrical designs can be seen clearly on her red dress.

72|73

Sakteng dances

The dances and festivals of the Sakteng valley are based on its own special traditions. Photograph 72 shows a dance with masks and costumes resembling those of the *Ace Lhamo* in Tibet. In photograph 73, in the foreground on the left, can be seen an *atsara*, a clown recognizable by his red mask. A richly-dressed image, representing a goddess, is mounted on a yak made of black rainproof blankets and a horned mask.

The hours and the days

74 Ploughing in Paro

75 Young girl with a spindle

76 Weaver at work

77 Bhutanese *menzimatra* cloth

78 Ceremonial teapot

79 Goldsmith finishing a *jachung*

80 Goldsmith finishing a teapot

81 Making ritual cakes (*tormas*)

83 Monk making *tsatsas*

85 Pupils at the school of painting

86 Small boy with slate

87   Prayer flag ready to be set up

88
Prayer flag

83

Monk making *tsatsas*
Tsatsas are small clay models that may represent divinities, or, like those shown in the photograph, be made in the shape of a chorten. They are generally painted red, gold or white. Placed in the temples, on prayer walls, in chortens and on portable altars, they have a votive function and are ordered in great quantities by pious believers. The ashes of the dead are customarily collected to be mixed with the clay for *tsatsas*.

84

Sculptors
A large number of statues, always representing some religious subject, are modelled from clay and then painted. Like the goldsmiths, the sculptors are grouped together in a workshop under the direction of a master. The statues are generally modelled on a wooden filler. Larger pieces are made in several parts. Certain details and decorations are cast in a mould and subsequently attached to the main body of the statue.

85

Pupils at the school of painting

86

Small boy with slate
The government has created a school of painting to prevent the traditional designs and techniques from dying out. All these young students already have a considerable mastery of draughtsmanship, and practise for hours repeating the same design, here clouds, that they must execute by following the iconographical rules very strictly.

87

A prayer flag ready to be set up
This is a relatively common sight. A small religious ceremony usually marks the erection of the flag.

88

Prayer flag

7

Festivals and dances

MANY FESTIVALS ARE CELEBRATED in Bhutan. Most are religious festivals where dances with a symbolic and didactic content are performed by both monks and laymen. For the Bhutanese, these festivals are unique occasions to prove their religious fervour, but also, decked out in their smartest clothes, to exchange the latest news.

The religious festival called *tshechu* is one of the most popular. It is celebrated in all the dzongs and in many of the temples to commemorate the different events in the life of Guru Rinpoche. (The photographs illustrating the tshechu in this book were taken at the Thimphu and Wangdiphodrang Tshechus.) The festival's dates, length and programme vary from one place to another, and furthermore, the programme is not fixed once and for all: dances may be added or omitted. Although certain dances are specific to certain places, most dances are performed all over the country, and are extremely popular.

Festive days of a secular nature such as the coronation, national day, etc., also retain a religious character. Monks bless the day, which is chosen because it is auspicious, and religious dances are performed before large crowds of people, who are fed at the Government's expense. The King himself, following a tradition instituted by his forefathers, mixes with his subjects, serves them, and takes part in many games and dances.

39 Orchestra of the Royal Dance Troupe

Dance of the drummers of Dramitse   90
(*dramitse ngacham*)

91 *Nubi Shey* dance at the coronation

92 Royal servants at the coronation

93 "Black Hat" dancer (*shanag)*

94 Dance of the Masters of the Cremation Grounds (*durdag*)

95   Dance of the Fearsome Gods (*tungam*)

96 Dance of the Judgement of the Dead (*raksha mancham*)

97 Dancer resting

98 Red mask of a fearsome divinity

99 *Atsara*, a clown, joking with the crowd

100 Midday-meal interlude at the Wangdiphodrang Tshechu

89

Orchestra of the Royal Dance Troupe

This is the orchestra of the Royal Dance Troupe, founded by the late King. It includes all the traditional Bhutanese instruments, from left to right, the flute (*zulim*), a kind of viol with four strings (*piwang*), a xylophone (*yangci*), and a seven-stringed lute (*dranyen*), whose belly is generally painted with religious or floral designs, and whose neck ends in the head of a stag, a horse, or a *chusin*, (*makara* in sanskrit) a marine monster. The instruments can be played solo, or used to accompany a song, as is the case here. The musicians are wearing traditional boots made of leather and coloured felt and a *go* of raw silk, decorated with a design called *lungsem*.

90

Dance of the drummers from Dramitse (*dramitse ngacham*)

This man with the mask of a dog is one of the 16 dancers in animal masks performing the Dance of the drummers from Dramitse whose choreography is particularly striking.

A monk related to the saint Pema Lingpa (1450-1521) lived in the monastery of Dramitse in eastern Bhutan. Transported in a vision to the celestial palace of Guru Rinpoche, he saw this dance being performed by the followers of the Guru. Since then, the dance has become very popular in Bhutan. It shows the victory of the Buddhist religion over the demons, and the sound of the drum symbolizes the essence of the religion which cannot be tangibly represented.

91|92

Coronation Festival

The festivities marking the coronation of His Majesty Jigme Singye Wangchuck took place in June 1974. Part of the ceremonies took place in the impressive Tashichho Dzong in Thimphu. As well as all the dignitaries of the kingdom, numerous Heads of State, ambassadors and other guests were present. Many religious dances and folk-dances were performed on this occasion. Photograph 91 shows a folk-dance called *Nubi Shey*.
All official ceremonies in Bhutan are accompanied by the offering of butter tea, or *seudja*, as well as other traditional drinks and dishes. On the occasion of the coronation, these dishes, served in richly adorned silver teapots and jars, were carried by a procession of royal servants called *chankhaps* (photograph 92).

93

"Black Hat" dancer (*shanag*)

The Dance of the Black Hats is one of the most beautiful of the religious dances. It is performed by monks robed in sumptuous brocades and wearing the famous black hat that gives its name to the dance. The front of their costume is covered by a magnificent apron decorated with a frightening face, grinning skulls and thunderbolts, or *dorje*, one of the symbols of tantric Buddhism. This dance has a double meaning: it commemorates the assassination in A.D. 842 of the Tibetan king Langdarma, the persecutor of Buddhism, by a monk who was wearing a black robe, and who had hidden his bow and arrows in the folds of his long sleeves. The dance also marks the possession of the dance area by the tantrists, so that they may subjugate and propitiate the deities of the earth. It is said that this dance was performed by the Shabdrung himself, which adds to its importance.

94

Dance of the Masters of the Cremation Grounds (durdag)

The Cremation Grounds, where men can ponder on the laws of impermanence are considered by the tantrists as privileged places of meditation. The Masters of the Cremation Grounds are protective deities who live in these places, which are symbolically situated on the periphery of the cosmic diagram (or mandala), where the gods of the tantric cycles live. Their function is to protect the gods by making harmless the evil spirits who might try to attack them. Their highly evocative costume makes them appear as representatives of a world where life and death merge and where fleshly appearance is only an illusion. The durdags bring on a piece of cloth a triangular black box in which lies a paste figurine which symbolizes the evil spirits.

95

Dance of the Fearsome Gods (tungam)

This dance, called tungam, often follows the dance of the Masters of the Cremation Grounds. Its significance is profoundly symbolic. Since certain evil spirits cannot be subdued by peaceful means, Guru Rinpoche and his followers take on a terrible aspect and destroy them. The dancers, sword in hand, whirl round, forming a circle that comes closer to the figurine lying in the black box. With this movement, they gradually encircle the evil forces in the figurine, which, at the end of the dance, becomes the object of a ritual murder, carried out with a magic dagger, the phurbu. The murder delivers the world from these evil forces and at the same time saves them, because it prevents them from continuing their misdeeds.

The incense carrier and the two musicians playing in the shawm are often present at the beginning of the dances.

96

Dance of the Judgement of the Dead (raksha mancham)

The Dance of the Judgement of the Dead is a kind of choreographed play, whose aim is both didactic and educative: it shows the characters whom every Bhutanese will meet after his death, and teaches him not to fear them. Moreover, it shows the importance of the good or bad deeds committed during earthly life, the karma, on which rebirth with a good or bad destiny depends. The large puppet represents Shinje Choegyel, the King of the Dead. He presides at the judgement of all beings, surrounded by his entourage of rakshas, beings with animal heads who act as judges. Dancing in front of Shinje Choegyel, the black demon and the white god hold black and white ribbons, attached to the crown of the Lord of the Dead. The white god and the black demon are born at the same time as every human being, and act as guardian angel and evil angel for him. At the time of judgement, the white god boasts of the merits of the accused, while the black demon emphasizes his faults. Each has corresponding white or black pebbles, which represent the actions of the accused and which are weighed in a balance. Shinje Choegyel, with the help of his magic mirror of truth, has the final decision on the fate of the accused.

97

Dancer resting

Under their mask, which they take off as soon as the dance is finished, the dancers wear a long strip of cloth that is rolled around the head and covers the lower part of the face. This material protects them from the injuries they might sustain from the masks during the violent movements of the dances. The coloured brocades of which the costumes are made traditionally come from China.

98

Red mask of a fearsome divinity
This dancer, a monk, waits while a friend fastens on his mask, showing a fearsome divinity. Many of the masks are made of painted wood, but some are also made in papier maché. The dancers look out of the mouth, rather than the eyes of the mask and the same masks can be used in different dances to represent different deities. The significance of the mask depends on that of the dance.

99

Atsara, a clown, joking with the crowd
The *atsaras* are among the most popular characters at the tshechus. Their name comes from the Sanskrit word *acarya,* and they are supposed to represent the Indian masters who might be reincarnated among us in this guise. The *atsaras* are clowns who amuse the crowds with their jokes and their crude behaviour. They relieve the atmosphere between dances, but they also love to mimic the dancers' gestures. No one is spared by their irreverent remarks. The most typical *atsara* mask, though there are

others, is the kind seen in this photograph: red with a large prominent nose.

100

Midday-meal interlude at the Wangdiphodrang Tshechu
The dances at festivals last all day, and the Bhutanese bring picnics in little baskets called *banchung.* These containers are made of two symmetrical baskets of woven bamboo in two layers, one in undyed strips, and the other with coloured strips in geometrical patterns. The two baskets fit into each other perfectly and enclose food, though not liquids, hermetically. Once they are opened, the two baskets are used as plates. The meal carried in the *banchung* for picnics generally consists of rice, dried meat and chillies. Small wooden bowls are used to drink butter tea and various alcohols, like *chang* and *arak,* which lend to the festive spirit. There are usually no dishes with gravy, for they are too difficult to transport. At home, the Bhutanese eat an enormous quantity of rice, accompanied by *tsems,* also served in little wooden bowls. The *tsems* are vegetables with chilli sauce, or even chilli peppers on their own, cooked with melted cheese, which is the national dish, *ema datsi.* Meat, preferably pork or yak, dried or fresh, is also cooked with chilli peppers and eaten with rice. The variety of rice that forms the most popular Bhutanese diet is a

variety with dark pink rounded grains commonly known as "red rice" which grows in the flooded paddy fields. Although in poorer regions, and at higher altitudes, eating rice is becoming more common, the staple of the diet there is still cakes made of buckwheat, wheat or barley flour, or maize ground into small particles and boiled like rice. Cheese made from the milk of the yak is eaten in small, hard, dried cubes and is much appreciated between meals.

The Bhutanese eat few fruits and almost nothing sweet. Their favourite beverages are salted tea with butter, *chang,* which is barley or millet beer, and *arak,* a stronger alcohol that is made by distilling *chang.*

All meals end with the handing out of *doma,* the areca nut coated with lime and wrapped in a betel leaf. The nut and the leaves are kept in rectangular silver boxes, and the lime in a round matching box. No cutlery is used. The Bhutanese eat with their right hand, and if they need to cut an item of food, they use the large knife that the men always carry with them.

8

The people of Bhutan

ANY ATTEMPT TO PORTRAY A PEOPLE has to grapple with the possibility that the inevitable over-simplifications involved may convey a false impression of them. But it would be a pity to miss an opportunity to describe such engaging people as the Bhutanese simply for fear of presenting a distorted picture. Fully aware of the pitfalls involved, we will attempt here to describe them through the invaluable medium of photographs.

It is worth beginning with the comments of a traveller. When Bogle visited the country on a mission in 1774, he wrote: "The simplicity of their manners, their slight intercourse with strangers, and a strong sense of religion, preserve the Bhutanese from many vices to which more polished nations are addicted. They are strangers to falsehood and ingratitude. Theft, and every other species of dishonesty to which the lust of money gives birth, are little known" (Markham, 1879, p. 37).

In 1983, these observations still hold true. One of the character traits that most strikes a visitor among the Bhutanese is the simplicity of their manners, together with their common sense and an uncommon consideration for others. Since the country was never colonized, and remained for so long isolated from the rest of the world, the Bhutanese have no complexes with regard to other peoples. They are what they are, with quiet pride.

While proud of their traditions, their political system and their religion, they are without arrogance. Indeed, in a country where each individual's place in society is accepted by everyone, there is no need to boast of one's parentage.

The Bhutanese live in a society which is organized in a complex hierarchy and governed by a rigorous etiquette, and they behave in a formal and respectful manner towards their superiors.

But when people of the same rank gather together, they are full of good spirits, uninhibited in expressing themselves and ready for all sorts of jokes.

The traditional gift of the *doma*, an areca nut coated in lime wrapped in a betel leaf, the piper betel, is an act of courtesy to a friend and a mark of hospitality. The Bhutanese are "bons vivants" who enjoy eating and drinking well, making the most of life. Any excuse can be made into an occasion for dancing, singing, archery, playing darts and stone pitching.

The adverse side of this agreeable picture is the rigour of everyday life, which, for 90 percent of the population, consists of hard labour in the fields and the tending of animals without the help of what we call mechanical progress. Agricultural equipment is very simple, and electricity and running water are still unknown in most villages.

Despite all this, the irrepressible good nature of the Bhutanese is always present: work in the fields and building houses is enlivened by singing, and mocking laughter and mischievous sarcasm punctuate every instant of life.

Like all true peasants, the Bhutanese are blessed with solid common sense, a certain instinct for disguising their real wealth, and an easily awakened sense of cunning. They live mainly in households that include several generations and different branches of one family. Men and women share the work, and the women are now contributing more and more to the family income with supplementary activities like weaving and shopkeeping. The men are not above looking after the children, and showing their affection for them. The opinion of the family plays an important role in all decisions. Divorce and remarriage are fairly frequent and inevitably entail complications over the division of wealth. This often necessitates litigation, as do the complex problems of inheritance, and the courts are always busy.

The pervasive spirit of tolerance, foreign to many other Asian countries, can probably be attributed to the influence of Buddhism. The Bhutanese are in general very religious, and signs of their faith mark the landscape: temples, monasteries, chortens and prayer flags. Each major event (birth, marriage and death, but also voyages, promotions, illnesses, construction work, and the annual blessing of the household) is celebrated by a religious ceremony either at home of in the nearest temple. Even the poorest houses have, if not a special room, at least an altar set with a few pious pictures, books, flowers and offerings to the gods. Pilgrimage to holy places and visits to the great lamas are part of the religious obligations of each individual.

The following photographs will help to fill out this impressionistic portait of the Bhutanese.

101
A family visiting the monastery

102 Archers around the target

103 Major Rinzin prepares to shoot

104 Dasho Adap Sangye

105 Three Bhutanese

106 A jovial old man

107 Old woman

108 Young woman with child

109 Young girl with hat

110 Fern-cross seller

111 Small boy with a basket of cheeses

112   Schoolgirl

Small boy   113

101

A family visiting the monastery

In the past, every family was expected to entrust one of its children to a monastery: it was at the same time a way of gaining merit and of providing an education for the child. Today, though the practice is less widespread, many particularly religious families still send one of their children to a monastery. From time to time, the family visits the child, which is placed under the tutelage of an older monk.

In this photo, the child monk is surrounded by his family, probably of humble status. The woman has her hair cut short in the traditional manner. She is dressed in the *kira*, a long piece of cloth wrapped around the body and which is attached to the shoulders by a pair of silver brooches, the *komas*, and at the waist by a wide belt, the *kera*. A small jacket, called the *toego*, is usually worn over the *kira*. The woman has thrown over her left shoulder the ceremonial scarf for women, the *rapchu*, which they must wear in order to enter dzongs and monasteries.

The two men are wearing the *go*, the male dress, a long and ample robe that is hitched up as far as the knees and held in place with a narrow belt. In his left hand, the old man is holding a rosary, which he uses to count the number of his prayers.

102|103

Archery

The Bhutanese are good sportsmen. Trained from their earliest youth to walk in the mountains, they are naturally sturdy. Besides football, the only foreign sport which is popular, they play many traditional games: throwing darts, putting the shot - a stone - and wrestling. The national sport, however, is archery, which is accompanied by a whole ritual of chants and dances and verbal encouragements. The target is placed at about 130 metres from the archers, who are divided into two teams and who may each use two arrows. The target is surrounded by the team of the archer, who avoid the arrows with diabolical precision and skill. If the arrow of their team-mate hits the bull's eye, they dance and sing around the target. Like the arrows, the bows are made of bamboo and require great physical strength, as well as great skill. Archery is an exclusively male sport, and a woman may not touch the bows without bringing bad luck. However, women do come to the tournaments, dancing and singing sarcastic refrains about the archers. Photo 103 shows Major Rinzin ready to shoot. He stands in the particular position that is called for in Bhutanese archery: his torso bent forward and the bow pointed towards the sky. In photograph 102, the archers who have already

shot stand around the narrow target, which is decorated with traditional designs, and watch the next arrow arrive.

104

Dasho Adap Sangye

Dasho Adap Sangye was a *Dzongda*, or district administrator. Under his *go*, he is wearing the formal white shirt, whose sleeves are turned up over those of the *go*. The red colour of the long scarf, the *kamni*, which he wears over his shoulder, symbolizes his status of *Dasho* (similar to Sir). This title is conferred by the king and entitles its bearer to wear a red scarf and carry a sword, the *patang*. Like the *rapchu* for women, the *kamni* must be worn in dzongs, temples and at certain official ceremonies. The small dog is an apsc, one of the breeds most prized by the Bhutanese.

Three Bhutanese
These three men are wearing the white scarf worn by the common people

A jovial old man
The design on the *go* of this jolly old man is a typical one called *pantsi*. Like many Bhutanese, he is carrying, in the pouch formed by the ample robe, several objects useful to him in everyday life: a knife, boxes for betel and lime, a small tea bowl and so on.

Old woman
This old woman is wearing the typical hat worn by women of the Paro and Haa valleys.

Young woman with child
This photograph shows very well the brooches used to hold the *kira* in place. The baby is wrapped in a blanket of harmonious colours made from a long roll of handwoven wool, the *yatra*, which is a speciality of the region of Bumthang. One of these rolls is carried in the bag that the woman has put down beside her. The bag itself is also made of handwoven cotton.

Young girl with hat
This girl is wearing the typical hat of the districts of Tongsa, Bumthang and especially Kheng. It is made from strips of bamboo and is composed of three layers. The first, not visible here, is woven into three-strand checks, and serves as a base for a layer of long strips, covered in turn by the third and uppermost layer, which is similar to the first layer, but woven from finer strips in a tighter weave (Montmollin, Marceline de, *Collection du Bhoutan: catalogue*, p. 134).

Fern-cross seller
One of the most highly-rated vegetables in Bhutan is without doubt the *nake*, a fern for which the high season is April, May and June. This vegetable is not cultivated, but is picked in forests throughout Bhutan, where it grows in the wild.

Small boy with a basket of cheeses
The most popular way of preparing vegetables in Bhutan is to cook them in a cheese sauce. *Datsi*, small soft white cheeses made from cow's milk, are not eaten as they are but added in small lumps to the vegetable as they finish cooking, making a delicious sauce.

Schoolgirl   Small boy
A very large number of girls go to school. Boys and girls have equal educational opportunities in Bhutan.

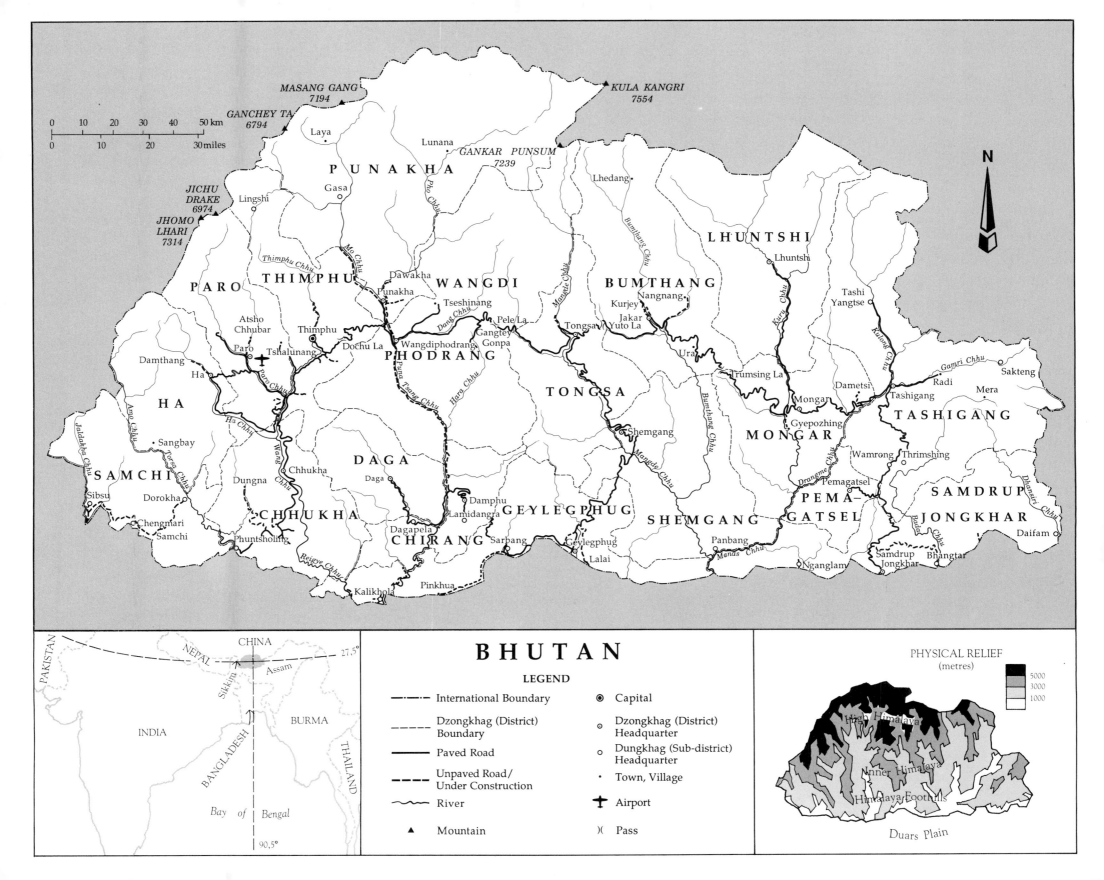

BHUTAN

LEGEND

- –·–·– International Boundary
- – – – Dzongkhag (District) Boundary
- ——— Paved Road
- – – – Unpaved Road/ Under Construction
- ∿∿∿ River
- ▲ Mountain

- ⊙ Capital
- ◎ Dzongkhag (District) Headquarter
- ○ Dungkhag (Sub-district) Headquarter
- · Town, Village
- ✈ Airport
-)(Pass

PHYSICAL RELIEF
(metres)

■	5000
▒	3000
□	1000

High Himalaya

Inner Himalaya

Himalaya Foothills

Duars Plain

PAKISTAN
CHINA
NEPAL
Sikkim
Assam
27,5°
INDIA
BANGLADESH
BURMA
THAILAND
Bay of Bengal
90,5°

Map labels

MASANG GANG 7194
GANCHEY TA 6794
KULA KANGRI 7554
JICHU DRAKE 6974
JHOMO LHARI 7314
GANKAR PUNSUM 7239

Laya
Lunana
Lhedang
Lingshi
PUNAKHA
Gasa
LHUNTSHI
Lhuntshi
Tashi Yangtse
PARO
THIMPHU
Dawakha
WANGDI
BUMTHANG
Atsho
Chhubar
Thimphu
Punakha
Tseshinang
Kurjey
Nangnang
Jakar
Yuto La
Kurtong Chhu
Paro
Tshalunang
Dochu La
Pele La
Gangtey Gonpa
Tongsa
Ura
Radi
Mera
Sakteng
Damthang
Ha
Wangdiphodrang
PHODRANG
Trumsing La
Dametsi
TASHIGANG
Tashigang
HA
Sangbay
TONGSA
Mongar
Gyepozhing
MONGAR
Wamrong
Thrimshing
SAMCHI
Dungna
DAGA
Chhukha
Daga
Shemgang
Temagatsel
SAMDRUP
Sibsu
Dorokha
CHHUKHA
Damphu
Lamidangra
GEYLEGPHUG
SHEMGANG
PEMA-GATSEL
JONGKHAR
Chengmari
Samchi
Dagapela
CHIRANG
Sarpang
Geylegphug
Panbang
Daifam
Phuntsholing
Lalai
Nganglam
Samdrup Jongkhar
Bhangtar
Kalikhola
Pinkhua

Rivers
Thimphu Chhu
Mo Chhu
Pho Chhu
Bumthang Chhu
Dang Chhu
Mangde Chhu
Kuru Chhu
Gamri Chhu
Puna Tsang Chhu
Hara Chhu
Paro Chhu
Ha Chhu
Amo Chhu
Wang Chhu
Torsa Chhu
Jaldhaka Chhu
Mangde Chhu
Bumthang Chhu
Drangme Chhu
Dhansiri Chhu
Bada Chhu
Manas Chhu
Reigye Chhu

Select Bibliography

Aris, Michael
Bhutan: The Early History of a Himalayan Kingdom.
Warminster, 1979.
ibid.
Views of Medieval Bhutan, The Diary and Drawings of Samuel Davis, 1783.
London/Washington, 1982.
Asian Cultural Centre for UNESCO
Bhutan, in *Asian Culture*, Summer/ Autumn 1983 No. 35, Tokyo, 1983.
Blanc, Ph.
Tibet vivant: Bhoutan, Sikkim, Ladakh.
Paris, 1978.
Bogle, George
See: Markham, Clements R.
Bonn, Gisela
Star auf der Asiatischen Bühne in *Indo-Asia*, 2, 1983, pp 6-20.

ibid.
Im Einklang mit dem Universum in *Merian*, 11/38, 1985, pp 88-97.
Bose, Kishen Kant
See: Eden, Ashley.
Coelho, V.H.
Sikkim and Bhutan.
Indian Council for Cultural Relations, Delhi, 1970.
Dago Tshering (ed.)
Bhutan: Himalayan Kingdom.
Published by the Royal Government of the Kingdom of Bhutan, 1979.
Das, Nirmala
The Dragon Country.
New Delhi, 1973.
Deb, Arabinda
Bhutan and India. A Study in Frontier Political Relations (1772-1865).
Calcutta, 1976.
Dowman, Keith (tr.)
The Divine Mad Man. The Sublime Life and Songs of Drukpa Kunley.
London, 1980.
DRUK LOSEL, Quarterly Publication, published by the Department of Information, Royal Government of Bhutan, Thimphu.
Eden, Ashley
Political Missions to Bootan, comprising the reports of the Hon'ble Ashley Eden, 1864, Capt. R.B. Pemberton, 1837, 1838, with Dr. W. Griffith's Journal, and the account by Baboo Kishen Kant Bose.
Calcutta, 1865. (Reprint: New Delhi, 1972, with the addition of Anonymous, *The Truth about Bootan by one who knows it*, originally published Calcutta, 1865.)

Griffith, William
Journal of Travels in Assam, Burma, Bootan, Afganistan and the neighbouring countries. Calcutta, 1847 (Chapters XI, XII, and XIII reprinted under the title: *Bhutan 1837-1838.* Kathmandu, 1975).
ibid.
See: Eden, Ashley
Haab, Armin
Bhutan, Fürstenstaat am Götterthron.
Gütersloh, 1969.
Haas, E.
Himalayan Pilgrimage.
New York, 1978.
Hasrat, Bikrama Jit
History of Bhutan: Land of the Peaceful Dragon.
Education Department, Royal Government of Bhutan, Thimphu, 1980.
Imaeda Yoshiro and Doffu Drukpa
Tashigomang of Bhutan.
Tokyo, 1982.
Karan, Pradyumna P.
Bhutan: A Physical and Cultural Geography.
Lexington, 1967.
Kohli, Manorama
India and Bhutan. A Study in Interrelations 1772-1910.
New Delhi, 1982.
Komatsu, Yoshio
Būtan. Ryū no ko Tinlei (Bhutan. Thinley, son of Dragon). Tokyo, 1986.
KUENSEL, News Bulletin (weekly), published by the Department of Information, Royal Goverment of Bhutan, Thimphu.
Labh, Kapileshwar
India and Bhutan. New Delhi, 1974.

Markus, U., Gansser, A., Olschak, B.C.
Bhutan, Königsreich im Himalaya.
Freiburg im Breisgau, 1983.

Markham, Clements R. (ed.)
Narratives of the mission of George Bogle to Tibet and of the journey of Thomas Manning to Lhasa.
London, 1879 (Reprint: New Delhi, 1971).

Mehra, G.N.
Bhutan: Land of the Peaceful Dragon.
Delhi, 1974.

Mele, Pietro Francesco
Bhutan.
New Delhi, 1982.

Montmollin, Marceline de
Bhoutan: Pays du Dragon.
Guide Artou, Genève, 1981.

ibid.
Collection du Bhoutan: Catalogue
(Extrait de *Etudes Asiatiques,*
XXXV-2, 1981).
Musée d'ethnographie,
Neuchâtel, 1982.

Nakao Sasuke
Hikyō Būtan (Bhutan unexplored).
Tokyo, 1959 (Reprint: Tokyo, 1971).

Nakao, Sasuke and Nishioka, Keiji
Flowers of Bhutan.
Tokyo, 1984.

NHK Filming Team
Harukanaru Būtan (Faraway Bhutan).
Tokyo, 1983.

Nishioka Keiji and Satoko
Shinpi no ōkoku (Mysterious Kingdom).
Tokyo, 1978.

Olschak, Blanche C. and A. Gansser
Bhutan: Land of Hidden Treasures.
London/New York/New Delhi, 1971.

Olschak, Blanche C.
Ancient Bhutan. A Study on Early Buddhism in the Himalayas.
Swiss Foundation for Alpine Research,
Zurich, 1979.

Peissel, Michel
Lords and Lamas.
London, 1970.

ibid.
Bhoutan, Royaume d'Asie inconnu.
Paris, 1971 (Reprint Genève 1988).

Pemberton, R. Boileau
Report on Bootan.
Calcutta, 1839 (Reprint: New Delhi, 1976).

ibid.
See: Eden, Ashley

Planning Commission, Royal Government of Bhutan
Bhutan. Country Economic Memorandum,
vol. I Main Report.
Thimphu, 1983.

Rahul, Ram
Modern Bhutan.
Delhi, 1971.

Rathore, L.S.
The Changing Bhutan.
New Delhi, 1971.

Rennie, David Field
Bhotan and the Story of the Dooar War.
London, 1866 (Reprint: New Delhi, 1970).

Ronaldshay, Earl of
Lands of the Thunderbolt: Sikkim, Chumbie and Bhutan.
London, 1923
(Reprinted under the title of
Himalayan Bhutan, Sikhim & Tibet,
Delhi, 1977).

Rose, Leo E.
The Politics of Bhutan.
New York, 1977.

Rustomji, Nari
Enchanted Frontiers: Sikkim, Bhutan and India's North-Eastern Borderlands.
Calcutta, 1973.

ibid.
Bhutan, the Dragon Kingdom in Crisis.
New Delhi, 1978.

Singh, Madanjeet
Himalayan Art.
London, 1968.

Singh, Nagendra
Bhutan, a Kingdom in the Himalayas.
A Study of the Land, its People and their Government.
New Delhi, 1978.

Stein, R.A. (tr.)
Vie et chants de 'Brug-pa Kun-legs le Yogin.
Paris, 1972.

Tōgō Fumihiko
Himaraya no ōkoku Būtan (Bhutan: Himalayan Kingdom).
Tokyo, 1965.

Turner, Samuel
An Account of Embassy to the Court of the Teshoo Lama in Tibet: Containing a Narrative of a Journey through Bootan, and Part of Tibet.
London, 1800 (Reprint: New Delhi, 1971).

White, J. Claude
Sikkim and Bhutan: Twenty-one Years of the North-East Frontier, 1887-1908.
London, 1909 (Reprint: Delhi, 1971).

List of illustrations